CINDERBITER

ALSO BY MARTIN SHAW

On Myth and Culture

A Branch from the Lightning Tree: Ecstatic Myth and the Grace of Wildness
Snowy Tower: Parzival and the Wet Black Branch of Language
Scatterlings: Getting Claimed in the Age of Amnesia
The Night Wages
Wolf Milk: Chthonic Memory in the Deep Wild
Elk Bone Is a Bright Owl

Translation

Courting the Dawn: Poems of Lorca (with Stephan Harding)

ALSO BY TONY HOAGLAND

Poetry

Sweet Ruin
Donkey Gospel
What Narcissism Means to Me
Unincorporated Persons in the Late Honda Dynasty
Application for Release from the Dream
Recent Changes in the Vernacular
Priest Turned Therapist Treats Fear of God
Turn Up the Ocean

Essays

Real Sofistikashun: Essays on Poetry and Craft
Twenty Poems That Could Save America and Other Essays
The Art of Voice: Poetic Principles and Practice (with Kay Cosgrove)
The Underground Poetry Metro Transportation System for Souls:
Essays on the Cultural Life of Poetry

CINDERBITER

Celtic Poems

Versions by

Martin Shaw & Tony Hoagland

Graywolf Press

Some of these poems first appeared in the *Kenyon Review, Mississippi Review, New England Review, Orion, Poetry*, and *Poetry International*.

This publication is made possible, in part, by the voters of Minnesota through a Minnesota State Arts Board Operating Support grant, thanks to a legislative appropriation from the arts and cultural heritage fund. Significant support has also been provided by Target, the McKnight Foundation, the Lannan Foundation, the Amazon Literary Partnership, and other generous contributions from foundations, corporations, and individuals. To these organizations and individuals we offer our heartfelt thanks.

Published by Graywolf Press
212 Third Avenue North, Suite 485
Minneapolis, Minnesota 55401

www.graywolfpress.org

Published in the United States of America
Printed in Canada

ISBN 978-1-64445-027-7

4 6 8 10 11 9 7 5

Library of Congress Control Number: 2019949912

Cover design: Kapo Ng

Cover art: Sam Chung

CONTENTS

FOREWORD: SHAKING THE TREE

This book holds an indecent amount of joy for me, and a sharp grief that my dear partner in the enterprise, Tony Hoagland, is not here to share in its publication. The depth of the material had us barking ecstatically like seals, as if we were trafficking in rare jewels. Maybe we were.

A decade ago, Tony and I sat together outside a pub in the Welsh seaside town of Barmouth. After a week in the surrounding hills, we were enjoying the almost hallucinatory pleasure of a pint of Guinness whilst looking out over the Irish Sea. There was a plate of fish and chips we were picking at, and the sky was unrelentingly blue.

Tony made a typically unusual suggestion: that I allow him to have a go at turning a traditional story I had been working on into a poem with stanzas. He would take my words and give them a new choreography on the page. The story was called "Cinderbiter," and his suggestion seemed a fine idea. He took the rumpus and arranged it into lines. We liked what we saw, and the wider work you have in your hands began. Through a bleak autumn and winter, the lines flew back and forth: sometimes Tony would suggest an edit, or turn of phrase, and we proceeded. The visual arrangement of the words on the page are entirely his. There's something of an oral liveliness to the way the lines skip and twist in their stanzas.

It is a disservice to the vital work of translators to call these translations: they are not; they are versions. I'm primarily a storyteller, not a translator. Traditional oral storytellers work with a kind of reanimation of old bones, rather than the extraordinary sense of seance a translator can conjure. We storytellers do this by shaking the tree of language. Most of the longer poems in this collection don't have a distinct literary freeze frame, and the shorter lyric poems can mostly be located in Kenneth Hurlstone Jackson's fine book, *A Celtic Miscellany*. I have been stewed merrily in these stories and poems much of my life. They are part of me. The words were shaped in the contours of a Devon copse or a sprawl of crow over a Galway field. They are my bread and beer.

From Taliesin to Dafydd ap Gwilym to Dylan Thomas, Celtic poets rove the landscape: the byres, hillocks, and far-reaching horizons. Poets are scarecrows of words, fiends of divine encounter. They get thoroughly soaked. There'll be a love affair somewhere along the way, an encounter with a spirit, maybe even the clash of swords. When they sit at table that evening, and the village crowds in, you can be sure they'll have a story to tell.

For Tony and me, it was an unimaginable delight to listen in.

Martin Shaw
Devon
2020

CINDERBITER

Celtic Poems

CINDERBITER

from the northern folktale "Assipattle and the Muckle Mester Stoor Worm"

The gray churn, the salted bruise, the green bridle;
the seal-proud comb around Scotland's skulled coasts.

Near it there is a farm.

A resolute tump; the gull-shrill wind beats like medicine for a gummed ear.
The family bent sow-low to the ground, praying to the seed-gods,

all arrogance sliced clean with poverty's cleaver;
the trance of fieldwork claiming all up to the silvered line of the shore.

All but one.

Years before, the mother of the hut squatted out seven sons—
        sprouts, cubs, little hefties suckling on the soured teat;

sullen blonds wrapped dead-tight in the family inhibition.
All but one.

Six sons, dulled by necessity—butchered by weather.

In the frosted dark, six sons line up with father
to yoke themselves to earth-labor,

to kiss the cold of Saturn's cross.
—Crook-backed, scoured like rounded loaves.

• • •

But the seventh sleeps by the fire's embers,
so smeared by ash he seems more magpie than boy,

locks hedgehog thick with ash;
his mind, loosened
                        by the flame's incanting.

The boy is underground, adrift
in the poet's dark roots of silence.

Gilled, adept at the sea's pressures,
crab-firm in the indigo black.

Stories come

Squatting like lumps of coal
darkly bright in the Viking currents.

The green teeth of the sea flower him with sagas.
He befriends the bannocked moon.

He is lifted, giddily over high desert:
three years in the twigged circle of a condor.

His slow heart sends a drum-thump
through the tangled combustions of history.

Rain-dancing through time,

he is a god-torch, flickered on the cave wall, his haunch
rich with prophetic ochre.

And everywhere the snow falls.

• • •

Lazy, they say, watching his slow, tidal breathing.

They who crack the earth, day in, day out.
They who snake by in their gritty dedications.

They whose hands know the rough licks of cattle,
whose eyes know the hills pearled with rain.

They whose arms are blue
under the lambing snow.

There is an egg of hate, fat amongst his wheat-yellow siblings

They long to string him up in the red barn;
to hasten his passage through this life.

They are a rough crowd for the bard.

Every night, he stirs, becomes immense,
looming in front of the land-blasted family.

Myth telling.

Stories lurch out beyond the ken of local knowledge
Sun on their backs, desert baked.

Prophetic spurts come rapid
from his traveled jaw.

A mangling
word-byre.

Tundra snow and jaguar teeth
spill onto the floor
of the fire-flecked hut.

He swears when his time comes
he will rise with the hero-energy.

Father leans forward with proud fists
and scatters the grandeur.

Says a serpent will lick the underside of the moon
before that happens

All cackle, and relax gladly into the familiar atmosphere of hurt.

The ebony lump drifts off.

There is always a killing to do round the farm.

• • •

One night, guts of rain overturn on the farm.
The darkness malignant, tough like a beetle's coat.

Steel drops of water brace the farm's door.
Amongst the commotion sounds a rough knocking; something wants in.

Father announces his coming to whatever waits.
Dog barks; he coughs big and lively, and slouches to the shaking frame.

It is the king's messenger. Cloak fat with water,
royal broach ornate, golden blazed amongst his costume.

He sits by the fire and accepts thin soup. He is large with news.

There is a worm:
the muckle mester Stoor Worm,
the serpent of Missgarrd,
a horror
coiled like a hateful rope around this world.

The worm yawns
and salt drifts of wave assault the bright corn.

It breathes out
and blond hills become black feathers,
ash piles, charred memory.

Its vast head has moved north,
its scaled mass is just a few miles off shore.

We fear that great yawn, and the breath
that will wrench us from the pap of life.

Our king has called to the directions;
hurled bones up at Orion's belt, gazed at his own hand's mysteries;

called on the spaeman, the northern magician
who grins and says only killing will do:
killing fire with fire.

First, seven girls without bed-knowledge were found:
bound tough, splayed crude to the rocks

for the great head to extend its forked tongue
and gather them into its inner chambers.

This darkness has occurred more than once
until our people demanded some other way.

The hamlets are empty of womb-maidens
so the spaeman went to the wilderness

was entranced, bog-crazy, rolled in thistle and gorse
got damaged by the forces,

and came back with worrisome knowledge:

the death of this curse asks a high price:
a flesh-treasure

the giving of the king's own daughter
to the grey tongue of the worm:

"The king has announced
by this fire
that his daughter will marry

any man soul-broad enough
to take this serpent on;
to roar with a bull's pride of its death.

The wedding dowry will be the kingdom itself
and the old king's sword Sikkersnapper

given him by Odin.

My lord is the last of the old kings
the last
with a hand in that northern cosmos."

Thirty strong men were roused
by that invitation;
blood-gorged with the promise of gold.

But at that beach they blanched,
fell back,
and wet the sand with their piss.

My king has no faith
in men like that.

Now he takes his own sword, called Sikkersnapper,
from the chest behind the high table.
Like a true champion he has brayed out

that he will die in the foam
rather than give his daughter to the worm.

His boat is in a sheltered place tonight;
tomorrow morning at dawn he will sail out,
my king,
dragging a sword too heavy for his years.

So I travel the storm-line this night,
farm to farm
repeating the challenge to be great.

To claim a sovereign's heft;
to risk a sacrifice;

to reach the beach by dawn
and halt our king's suicide.

• • •

The rain-servant allows a murk of tears to mingle with his beard,
and will not wipe the drops away.

He rises, and returns to the shaking gale.
He has many miles still to ride.

The family slopes off to bed.
That's more excitement than has landed on the farm in long years.

Crescent-mooned in his charcoal nest, the boy hears
mother and father, turning it around in their pillow talk,

forgetful of the extra lugs sheltered in the gloom.

• • •

Mother wants to see the dawn reckoning.
If all is doom, they may as well get to see the show.

Father agrees, and reckons on Teetgong, their speediest horse
getting them to the beach early.

Mother raises herself onto one arm and asks
just how is it that he gets such speed out of the horse?

Like a mighty streak when aroused, a muscled blur over the gorse.
Ah, men have secrets. He turns under the blanket,

but she is insistent, offering all sorts of enticements.
Her hands raise a hard sweat, and soon he is adrift in confession:

"For Teetgong to stand
I clap his left shoulder;

to run, two claps on the right;

but when I want the black gallop
I bring out my fith-fath:
my cunning
my humors
my art
my sly magics.

Now to make his hooves carve hot soil,
I blow my thrapple

the windpipe of a goose
my fetish blower

that never leaves
my secret pocket."

She chews on this knowledge and straddles him.
Their cum-cries are muffled
by their hands clamped rough on each other's mouths.

Later, their hair mixed on the pillow,
with the burr of the big man's snoring;

and the boy crawls out of sight
to his father's brown coat, piled by the bed.

Inside is a pocket, hidden,
where his hand finds the thrapple, smooth and somehow warm.

This is the first of three great steals.

● ● ●

Out to the stables. The storming has passed.
Now it is fierce clear, sharp as an Irish knife.

Stars are ice-webbed on the blue curtain.

The horse rears up and kicks, till the boy
reaches out in the dark and pats Teetgong's left shoulder.

He stills and submits to the bridle.
As he pats the right shoulder, the horse surges forward and bellows.

Deep in himself, hawk-circling his well of memory,
the father hears the neigh and wakes.

Knowing that soul-din, that tender whinny,
from the beast nursed since foal on the green hill,
his heart directive, his appled-affection.

His hand reaches into the black slit of his pocket. Gone.

• • •

The family scatters from their sleeping piles.
Onto their beasts, half-dressed, stubbled like the field.

Father leads, his guttural language
drilling holes in the black air ahead of him.

Rat a tat tat.

He calls to his horse with all his slow wisdoms,
claims back all his countless hours of care,

for this hijack to cease, for his beast to come halt.

Hi, hi, ho
Teetgong wo!

It almost works.

• • •

But away—the rider's blood cooks
like red branches under his muck-skin,
his tongue dirk-sharp with the urging.

The horse tries to turn its head, desperate for the old calling,
but the Cinderbiter turns the magic against its owner,

and blows mad-hard on the thrapple.

With that sound the horse becomes an occult arrow;
flies beyond, far beyond the father and sons.

He could have galloped off the very edge of the world.

• • •

On through the night:
                the son on the stolen horse,
                        the father in the dark.

How many fathers and sons,
ride in the night like this?

Father behind father behind father.

Lonely like a Grendel.

• • •

Dawn is near as the boy reaches the beach.
Saddle-bashed, he clambers off.

Between the sea and the land is the thin strip of beach,
and on that beach, a tiny croft. He slips inside.

An old woman sleeps under a rough blanket, a cat at her feet.
The hut groans woozily in and out
as if it is she that breathes it.

The fire in excitement all night, an iron pot beside it.

As is his cinder-habit he gazes at the embers,
then scoops a lump of peat from the fire,

drops it quick in the pot and is off out with it.

He does not see it open, the one bright eye of the crone.
He does not see it open, the one green eye of the cat.

They steadily watch:
they have seen all this before.
Their eyes close.

This is the second of three great steals.

• • •

Air is chill, but dawn has come.

Close to shore, the king's boat rocking on its anchor.

A servant stands in the boat, so cold
he beats his arms on his chest to warm himself.

Cinderbiter shouts greeting
and pretends to dig a firepit for a breakfast of limpets;

then starts to yelp, and bellow—I see gold!
A glitter-harvest right here before me on the beach!

He squats in the half light and starts to dig,
whooping a treasure-chant to quicken the king's man.

The servant is over the wave, heading ashore, dripping,
then pushing the boy aside, snout in the dirt, paws churning as spades.

Quickly into the harsh tide, the boy wades.
The sun appears as a red ball over the land, and he lets anchor.

This is the third of three great steals.

• • •

Ahead is an island.
But that is no island.

The scaled-greasy-gray aquatic scalp of the serpent.

End-bringer
       Terror-wakener
              Black worm

Seven yawns the creature makes,
and then the tongue seeks flesh council,
darting the waves.

Our mottled dreamer aims the boat directly at it.

Raging on shore, the king's men gather, but then are stilled
staring at the loose-crow boy
                        with a crone's pot on a stolen boat.

They make crude bets for the swiftness of death's arrival.

On the third yawn, the betting gets hot:
the boat and boy are sucked on the green brine

slosh-quick down the throat of the beast.

The Underworld
The Belly of the Whale
The Flesh Labyrinth

It was a phosphorescent world
lit up from the inside,

with muscled tunnels, and surging, gurgling waters
taking him deeper and deeper.

Beyond chapel, holy books, tea leaves.

Have you your adventure now, Cinderbiter?

Is the dirt of the fields washed clean enough here for your poet's bones?

He does not look left or right, but is an intended arrow
and waits till the boat finally hits shallows.

Into the glowing murk, he splashes
And takes his dagger—his muckle-ragger—from his belt.

A sharp belly acid sloshes the walls; fierce stink drips
but he picks his pace like an Indian runner

in this subterranean luminosity
in this snake underground place.

He is here in his myth:

Bright-feathered Tammuz
Dagara grandfather
Mooroa Man
Tattorhood my goat sister
Run with me now, utterly.

Chaw Gully Raven
White Buffalo Woman
Pan of the shepherd's pleasure
Keep me firm, candle me with story.

Brave Tyr
One who places his hand
In the wolf Fenrir's mouth
See this small thing I do
In this Dragon Underworld.

Mabon
and Twrch Trwyth

Hunter and Hunted
vast tusked boar
agile pursuer
I call on both
keep me nimble.

The worm's liver he finds.

The muckle-ragger cuts into it, deep, livid and bloody.

Then from his swinging pail
he plants the crone's ember
in the splayed hole, the rupture.

His dreaming-breath puffs wildly and the ember roars up
again to flaming, charring, catching hold.

When the whole liver is smoking, he splashes the tunnel back to his boat.
The worm judders, wretches, starts to shape-lurch.

He is getting cooked.

The boat catches a stink of water from its belly,
and carves up time and space in its exit from the serpent.

Drenched in worm-foam, a black stick in the air—
the boat soars and lands,
hard and timber-blistered on the wet mud of the beach.

The boy is flung clear.

But the king and his men, the crone and her familiar,
even his gathered family, are only half-looking at him.

Because the world is changing.

The sky is a riot of black smoke from the worm's nostrils
Flood water from its gob loosens the waves.

With a terror-smash it lifts its great head, its tongue
shoots out and licks the underside of the moon,

its whole body stands and tries to hold on, in tremor now.

Above them all, the iron column of the beast goes mad-a-shake;
from its slathering mouth, the teeth spray out—

First tooth: the Orkneys
Second tooth: the Shetlands
Third tooth: the Faroes

Finally its body leaps back, far back, steaming into deeper waters,
coiled tight in a death-mass it passes.

Iceland it becomes
where the liver still smokes under burning mountains.

Over time the people gather their senses back.
Sky clears, the sun-gifted yellow beams.

Some great energy has passed close by,
but passed.

The king levels his gaze on the grimed-and-brined man,
this drifter into the center of trouble,
this magpie of the three steals.

And places the heft of Sikkersnapper into that seer's calm hands.
His family squints through the smoke, tiny-eyed.

Then she comes:

Bright daughter,
swan on the pool;
hot moon, strong curved;
a roving deer under God's stars.

Full voice, voice

that makes the
beehives golden,
dew lick the dark grass,
fire-spark at the anvil.

Green cloak,
brooch of fine white bronze,
grass does not bend
under her foot.

She is her own country.

Full-thighed, flower-arrayed.
She has budded slowly under the fur
of snowy winter.

Read by the yellow candle,
gathered sticks on the pagan hills.

Swum through a hundred acres
of whale-thought.

She knows what stands behind her.
She is an Owl-Wife, knowledged.

No mere reward, but strong-minded; kestrel-swift, a stinging honey.

Our scarecrow man is agreeable to her,
so different from those salted thugs of court.

There will be conversations for these two,
and bright-rimmed goblets
and a walled garden with tall pines.

The wedding will last for years.

DEIRDRE REMEMBERS A SCOTTISH GLEN

Irish, author unknown, possibly fourteenth century

Glen of my body's feeding:
crested breast of loveliest wheat,
glen of the thrusting lorn-horn cattle,
firm among the trysting bees.

Wild with cuckoo, thrush and blackbird,
and the frisky hind below the oak-thick ridge.
Green roof that covered a thousand foxes,
glen of wild garlic and watercress, and scarlet-berried rowan.
And badgers, delirious with sleep, heaped fat in dens
next to their burrowed young.

Glen sentried with blue-eyed hawks,
greenwood laced with sloe, apple, blackberry,
tight-crammed amid ridge and pointed peaks.
My glen of the star-tangled yews,
where hares would lope in the easy dew.

To remember is a ringing pain of brightness.

THE MANSION OF THE WOODS

Welsh, by Edmund Price, 1544–1623

I heard their larking only yesterday
the loquacious boys
of the green trees.

To me they are laureates,
a-flutter with god,
a high riot in the rafters.

Nightingale of the lovers;
blackbird loose with zeal;
woodlark adrift with wanton speech;
linnet preaching from the brake.

How can so much passion
be scattered on the emerald bow?

Near is the grove, sweetened by April
foot-deep with primrose, fat-hipped with clover
and the breasting milk of daisy.

Some shepherd's dreaming
must be templed thick
with the flowered hawthorn tip
and the silvered birch, in its womanly greening.

Buckle my knees
                by the fountain;
I must praise the champion's mouth

for the water's many turns: sing
of its brightness, its glinting calm,
melody and dreaming power.

And I come rough with my gods too,
my loving jaw and my earthy songs:

The Gentle Girl of Gwynedd
The Irish Girl, Comely Elir
The Horned Oxen
The Maiden's Laughter

Red beads from my mouth, these are—

In this glade, all is drawn up together,
intermingled, commingling;
the timbered palace of brown voice;
the glad fellows of the branch;
the voluminous plants, a gaggle in joy.

No trouble is here, no sickness;
Venus owns this Bright Mansion.

Drag to this place
all crippled in spirit
both young and old.

What strange bounty the Father sings!
His tone strong-backed with wheat,
and glimmered with barley
on the horn-clear hills.

This owling den
of day-gold singing
and blue praise
to the moon-wild sea,

is grace abounding.
A high warm song.

And ten young horses over the hill.

THE WILD MAN AND THE MONASTERY

Irish, author unknown, twelfth century

There was an age,
an age
when sweeter for me
than the hum of monks

was the coo-call
of the ringdove
flitting above
the gray pool.

An age when sweeter
than the tinkling call to prayer
was the blackbirds' warble

in the dusty gable
and the stag's dark belling
in the storm.

Sweeter than a woman
pressed thigh-close
was to hear, at matins,
the cry
of the heath-hen
alone on the moor.

Stuck in pews
with the priests' feeble bleat,
my feet roamed
with the splendid plainsong
of the wolf.

These fattened monks
are swift to ale,
but I like better

ice-water cupped
from the
green spring.

Though you may swell
with the drinking hall's
fatted meat,
I like better
the head of watercress

eaten in a place
scoured free from sorrow.

BARD-COME-A-FIRE

from Vita Merlini, *by Geoffrey of Monmouth, 1150*

It was then, in that time

that Myrddin—our Merlin—
drew wisdom and laws

from the nettle-grass and the horse chestnut
of South Wales.

He issued seership and instruction
to the proud Demeti.

He had the bracken ear,
the coltish tongue,
the dark speech
   required for such largeness of task.

His gleeful word
could school the temperament of young princes.

His curling language could lend a swan elegance.

Merlin.

Unflinching with truth.
Ordering a firm house in the roar of the court.

Son of an incubus,
he still claims residence
to some inner animal.

And he is friend
to the Old-Man-in-the-Fur-Coat—the bear.

He has gathered red berries by the cold stream,
he has pressed his mind
through gorse and hemlock.

To other men, his outer-being is calm:
but inside, he is rattled with knowing:
a ripping hail, a speech-blizzard carving up
the skull of his woken-ness.

Double-tongued is he:
faithful attendant both to the wolf's epiphany
and the politics of the long-house.

• • •

To Merlin, alone in his secret den,
this gut-black-power, this second sight
has brought a new worry.

Peredur of Wales,
prince of the Venedoti,

is drinking blood-buckets
from the veins of the people of Gwenddolau,

Britain sags with the keening.
The bruised hills hold a mother's terror,

the tree line is a blood-comb
from war's many bragging roosters.

The bone-hills fire up across the moor.

• • •

A battle is arranged, punctual.

Warrior gear a-gleam; straight turf and firm;
under foot, no bog: a good map for killing.

Merlin backs Peredur,
as does Rodarch, high man of Cumbria.

Merlin's brothers come too—three boars
tusk-drunk for the fight, chanting low behind him.

The good seer, Merlin, smeared thick with dirt and rook blood
struts a tawny mile in front of the soon-to-dying men.

He wants to raise a hail-storm in their souls.

He calls out the enemy:

May your hearts rip like bursting cliffs
May shit fill your veins
May your cocks shrivel
May your balls be lumped coal that never sires
May your bowels cluck with terror
at the sight of we western men,
we handsome destroyers.

May your eyes be as milk
and battle-blindness descend
leading you to the red pasture of Welsh blades.

May you feel good horror
at our bastard strength and our hoof-power.
May our anvil bludgeon
loose your feeble brain-mush
as compost for our noble soil.

Have at them.

This black father, Merlin,

hurls dark speech like warfare
and all his loving sons charge the field.

The three brothers of Merlin,
electrified by speech

seek the field's deepest trouble,
to be witnessed aflame by their men.

Fame will not come to those that don't.

But speech can be fragile.
As any man knows,
our best prayers may land
this side of the river.

In full view
the bold three are spitted;
are churned and gutted on those Scottish irons.

No parley, no dainties: no intricate bargain,
no parchment treaty;

just the red carve of weapon
and feet splash-buttered with crimson.

• • •

Carrion feed on both Welsh and woad,
lunatic-fierce the battle-smash of shield and blade.

But slowly the fighting turns in Peredur's favor;
with an agonized surge
the Welsh claim the day.

• • •

Merlin bears witness to this fleshy mash:
              this slash-tangle of young life
              chucked hard from its cage.

His eyes see the blue smoke of souls leaving bodies.
He cannot celebrate.

His part in their leaving
settles its hard weight round his brow:

a crown of dark bees weaving death-honey.

Peredur's fist claps on Merlin's shoulder
as apple-booze gullets the thirst of survivors.

Yet he cannot celebrate.

The seer haunches in the posture of a dog
—a hound aggrieved.

The magus is skewered on bewilderment;
ivy shackled in his brittle grief.

He flogs the red ground, still cherried with dying.

On foot and on fist he flees
till he finds forest's edge and plunges the green.

● ● ●

Merlin a-wild:

his way is not the hunter's bragging stride
but the subtle track of roe deer;

in summer's glades,
shadowed by the rowan,

its cleft hoof leads him toward upland pastures,
                    where they graze.

And he too grazes:
gnashes plant roots, aches with blackberries
plucks fruits of the bough.

But with the first hoar-frost
he tastes discontent,
and panics for survival.

"Holy maker,
Where are the acorn and the grasses?

Once I rested under nineteen apple trees,
lusty with fruit;

with your silvered cloaking
you have stolen these from me.

Your wet gales have pruned
their pagan garland,

left the old trees bald as a grove of monks,
a repenting forest.

In this iron soil if I find but one root,
I am shoved aside by wicked pigs.
The boar snatches my booty.

Now even my summer companion, the wolf,
hunts leftover dinner;

too broken to drag the goat into unknowing;
too weak to skirt the acorn field.

Celestial keeper,
do you hear my whinnies?"

Now the seer learns what it is
to be deep-wintered.
The white flakes settle in his beard.

• • •

At the top of a mountain
is a special spring.

The water crofted
by hazels and thick brush.

Here is Merlin's den, his world tree.
From this tree and in this spring
he can see as much as it is good for us to see.

Here cuckoo and nightingale coo in green speech
from the broad branch of the oak.

Brooks course here in a rabble song
through the mossy roots,
easing the damage of his soul-fractures.

Here, led by rumor, a lute player comes,
and sings of a wife and a sister

who ride weeping-horses
at the lack of a husband and a brother.
He sings of Merlin's old life.

One thread at a time, sly note by sly note
the singer plants the murmur in his heart,
remembering:

The hearth fire

The joyful tumble

A king's confirming gaze

Calmed now, restored,
Merlin is Merlin again.

Back to King Rodarch he follows the ballad singer.

With falcons, and hounds, and many swift horses
Rodarch swathes him with gifts:

gold Persian plates:
a cup hewn by Wayland the Smithy.

This is how a king brokers ownership;
then waggles iron chains if refused.

• • •

But Myrddin Emrys is too wild-touched,
too forested now to be kept.

His foliaged hair curls like a snake-den
His eyes roll back in his head

As the king pleads for his return,
the king's wife enters and greets her husband.

In Merlin's beholding

the king smiles and lifts gently
a leaf from her hair.

• • •

Merlin laughs to himself.

When asked, laughs again.

"How double single acts can be, my lord!
You are worthy of both praise and jest.

When from your woman's hair you pulled that leaf,
you proved more faithful to her than she

when she waited for her lover just now
to come and lay her in the old way
under the linden tree.

So, a cuckold may be king, or king a cuckold.

—Are you still sure?
Do you really seek a prophet at your ear?

I am one who sees.
I am the one who hears the seventy languages:

of dromedary's hoof and the secrets of wives;
of the black sea and the death-groans
of a feudal lord; of cowslip, foxglove
and the ice sheets of the north.

My gifts are not easily come by.
I strove hard to get them.

Now let me go."

● ● ●

Merlin a-wild.
He swims out past the bay of human affection.

Now no summering lament.
He enters the wood with vigor,

drives his body to a blue shape sculpted by wind.
Survives on crusts of frozen moss.

He does not miss the law-court,
nor the jokes of the marketplace.

• • •

One night, death-bringing cold sweeps away all cloud.

A good hawk, Merlin perches in his nest,
observing all the courses of the stars.

They remind him of the old life he has given up.

He was married once, then abandoned her,
Gwendolen, the long-suffering,

when he took the forest for his home.

It was the way the planets glittered that told him
of his wife's new love.

This night, that old story has a new chapter.

"Venus—I read your frosted message in the dark
as faithfully you follow down your consort sun.
My beak snaps at your heels with wonder.

I see another ray, that arcs from you,
the ray that splits lovers:
Gwendolen has bed-knowledge of another.

And the stars tell me of a wedding."

The strange man gazes up
at the yellow breast of the moon
                                    and he remembers.

• • •

As day breaks, Merlin begins his journey.
His brown legs straddle a mighty stag.

Behind him in the mist arrays
a cavalcade of tyned companions;
a roaring herd, tight with power.

Like sheep behind a shepherd, they follow him
—these utterly untamed things.

The drumming of their hooves like a heady wine
an earthy singing
announcing the bold.

In time they arrive at the wedding: a pretty scene.

Flowered maids and men drink water
and munch on cress.

From his place in the unconsecrated grasses,
the former husband bellows his raw greeting.

For just a second, a second—
a smirk ghosts over the bridegroom's face:

This wild thing, this tattered rustic
this marsh-remnant, this Enkidu,

this former owner of the property
—I have had his wife. And she loved it.

Now he who is no more the lover runs amok.
With guttural roaring Merlin wrenches

the antlers from his piss-blood stag;

its skull a gutting hemorrhage,
stars charging from the red eruptions,

legs bucking with immaculate suffering.

Those forked antlers—hurled like spears of bone,
splinter life at their impact.

Merrily they carve the groom-man's handsome face.
Seven tynes split his jaw, nose, eye, and brain.

His gaggling, dragged-out death upon the grasses
startles jackdaws from their nests.

Even his smoke-soul is blocked from leaving
by the thumb and forefinger of the magus,

forever trapped in some gray penitentiary.

The red spurt sprays the flowered circle.

Gwendolen
Gwendolen
Gwendolen

Even now I show my care.

The entourage turns,
and vanishes through the bleak hood of trees.

• • •

Now Merlin has a sister—one who is still loyal.
She follows his bone-white trail,

his moon over the water; his dream-beckoning.

She has built a home for him, out there:
Seventy doors, and seventy great windows

where he can study in the warmth of yellowed Phoebus, the sun.
Where he can deep-drink celestial arithmetic,

and plough through leafy drifts of knowledge;
where he will split his mind with the wet lightning of foresight.

His wintering has shown him the beauty of a candled hut.
So he slips in, like a thin man between autumn and winter.

Women scribes trained for diction attend him;
who stake his herding songs to parchment.

In this nest of woozy dreaming
he churns out prophecies:

"Gather—I gaze into the scrying bowl
of my mind, and I have news:

I see that Albion sinks deeper into madness:

Peace will be uprooted by the lust of Furies.
Dynasties, feudal battery, civil war.

The children of the Cornish Boar
will drag forth murder from the west.

I see the sea-wolf, come for sword-play, lay siege to Cirencester.
Through hut and meadow he will butcher.

Two hundred monks will die in Leicester;
Saxon kings will grip our green-boughed towns and hamlets.

This will go on for a long time.
Three dragons will wear three crowns.

Then French—the Normans, boated;
shingled-coat, and bladed, they will come.

Their ships headed at both bow and astern.
They shall be like terror-whores.

They will hew and yoke us,
sow nightmare into every crack and burr
of us: our speech, and thought,

our secret dens and leafed ambitions.
They will fully have us, as crows do worms.

I have spoken before of warring dragons
a-crackling fierce under our muck and stone.

They will cinder all that shunned my subtle tongue."

And so it goes. Day after day, in the crafty hut.
The drastic prophecies continue.

• • •

As the season moves, this wyrd-tongue finds its parchment home.

Merlin settles his feathers, and reaches out for good conversation,
to linger by the hearth side with some company.

In the winter Taliesin arrives; Taliesin, the sage.
Fresh from the side of Gildas the monk.

It is a rare sweetness, these two old men together—
Merlin and Taliesin, comparing universes.

This Taliesin, shapeshifter—who has been
a grain,
a salmon,
a floating babe in the sea,

tells Merlin of the nature
of wind and rain,

of the four elements,
of the triple order of heaven:

why the sea must be wet,
of an Island of Apples,
a Fortunate Island, ruled by eight sisters:

Morgen
Moronoe
Mazoe
Gliten
Glitonea
Gliton
Tyronoe
Thiten

The last is vast with music: Thiten of the song.

There they sit, these shape-leapers,
throwing history between them like a ball,
catching glints of their own story
in its smoky weight.

But suddenly
a servant comes with news:

a new spring has burst from the hillside;
a river of pure water.

The two men hurry to the unfolding.

Old Merlin drinks the full taste;
splashes his forehead. Weeps.

Some black dog rises from his side and pads away.

In the days that follow, suitors once more come for Merlin.
To pay him court, request
his leadership, to make a center for the realm.

But he points to an old oak.

"I saw the acorn from whence that sprang.
I laughed with the woodpecker as we watched
it grow. My sap, its sap, grow weak.

I am old, wee hen, I am old."

Wild swans flurry the lake.
It is dusk.

Then behind him, he hears a voice, it is his sister,
stepping into that clear light. It is her time now.

From the hut of the seventy doors, from the wide-open windows—
she starts a chant of knowledge.

Another age begins.

THE RUINS OF TIMOLEAGUE ABBEY

Irish, by Sean O'Coileain, 1814

I am gut-sad.

I am flirting
with the green waves,
wandering the sand,
feeding reflection
into the seaweed's foam.

That shaker's moon is up.
Crested by corn-colored stars
and traced by those witchy scribblers
who read the bone-smoke.

No wind at all—
no flutter
for foxglove or elm.

There is a church door.

In the time
when the people
of my hut lived,

there was eating and thinking dished out
to the poor and soul-sick
in this place.

I am in my remembering.

By the old frame of the door
is a crooked black bench.

It is oily with history
of the rumps of sages,

and the foot-sore
who lingered in the storm.

I am bent with weeping.
This blue dream
chucks the salt from me.

I remember
the walls god-bright
with the king's theology,

the slow chorus of the low bell,
the full hymn
of the byre and field.

Pathetic hut.
Rain-cracked and wind-straddled.
Your walls bare nubbed
by chill flagons of ocean spit.

The saints are scattered now.

The high arch
is an ivy tangle.
The stink of fox
is the only swinging incense.

There is no stew
for this arriving prodigal,
no candled bed.

My shape
is sloughed with grief.
No more red tree
between my thighs.
My eyes are milk.
Rage is my pony.

My kin lie under the ground
of this place.

My face has earnt
the grim mask.
My heart a husk.

But my hand. My hand
reaches through this sour air
and touches
the splendid darkness
of my deliverer.

HUT TALK

Irish, author unknown, eighth or ninth century

As I craft my ear to eternity,
dear has been my hut,
my silence, my pilgrim's seat.

I am still unripe,
and much-needed to be taken
from the village
to make holy my frame
with good habits.

I have stretched desire on the rack
and made my body feeble,
my bed cold and anxious.

Food to me is bondage.
I thin my blood with lack.
My bitter meal of dry bread
is weighed out strict.

Water is my drink
from the fair hillside,
where no abbots quaff.

I like that hollowed look.
Blemished, serene, leathered.

The gospels are my fire path
and psalms each hour.
Here is a final end
to the storyteller's winter chatter.

My knee is bent forever.
Seek me, creator,
in my twigged cathedral.

Alone, alone, alone.
I bed in with many graves.
My vice ground down
amongst the peat.

THE STARS

Welsh, by Dafydd ap Gwilym, fourteenth century

I have a reckless love.

It bids instruction to my feet,
and sends me long miles;

makes me crawl through
swamp and copse and bracken

to meet my generous woman.

Our hair tangles on the pillow;
her body a warm stable.

In May-time we rut right there
under the birch trees,

alive in the greenness of things;
the nightjars flickering

the heavy horses
alive alive in the orchard.

Kings of the Apple-Reign.

Yes, ours is a boastful love.

But last night was different.

A crisper evening
makes a many-miled walk
to my lover's hall.

Night-blind, night-blind I was.

My eyes were pulp on the pitch-black road,
ghoul-thin across the moor.

I was calling on Tristan,
that southern Hawk
who always found his chalk-white woman,

I careened like a gypsy, and lost the way.

So much for old stories.

I staggered about in mud-ridged fields.
Nine thickets caught my finger and jacket.

I gripped an ancient wall
like a sailor grips his oar
when he sees the storm coming.

Ahead was the brow of some terrible mountain,
thick with goblin, amok with caves;
a dungeon of my own making.

"Holy maker, I ask for bail;
in the speech of my people, I barter tonight:

if brought safe to my lover's hall,
I will pilgrimage to far Llanddwyn.

I am Ap Gwilym:
bring me bright path

and I will lower my head
to the babe that was born in the glow of animals."

The stars came out then,
brilliant and holy;
a gold foam to one without shelter.

Oh, a wild zodiac
laced the black roof of my becoming.

I spoke in a torch-blaze of naming:

Heaven's Bonfires

Cherry Sparked
Fox Fire

Glands of the Moon

Full Fruit of the Bronze-White Foam

Night's Candles

Hoare-Frost Scattering

Bone-Ground Circles

Hammered Shield-Rivets of the Sun

Pebbles of the Blue Stream

Longing's Half-Pennies

Saddle-Stones of the Black Riders

These stars
so high the wind cannot wash them,
embers from the Old God's blaze

a hundred altars
for the whinnying lovers
amok in the smoky dark.

This pure light
showed me the way on the muddied track,
the sluice-wet valley, the bruising rocks,

and I scampered on reprieve
—whetted, hot-backed
strange-blessed by a mossy Christ,

I come to the day-breaking door
of my true love's hall.

My friends;
I make no great display of my suffering,
no tinker's parade of my woe

but say this to my girl of the deep valley:

my keen-edged axe shall not strike twice
against the side of her rock!

THE GIRLS OF LLANBADORN

Welsh, by Dafydd ap Gwilym, fourteenth century

Since I was young I have been mad for girls.
One dozen times a day I fall in love.

No Sunday has passed but that I am in the pews at Mass,
in my feathered hat,

my eyes turned keen across the congregation.
But in this parish a curse from God has ruined me.

Neither gentle lass, nor lonely wife, nor cankered hag
will sport with me.

Among themselves, the women say, "View his face;
he has the look of one who knows sin well."

There never was a spell so persistent as this.

My neck has grown cricked from looking left and right,
and still no mate.

I am no more close to winning one of them
than if I was their enemy.

And I must give up these fantasies
and become a hermit, or even worse, a saint.

SNOW

Irish, author unknown, eleventh century
Welsh, by Dafydd ap Gwilym, fourteenth century

No world but white.

Even words of a girl
won't shift me from the peat-fire.

Here's what I say to her:
that I would arrive
as white as the clothes of a miller.

Not a grand look
for romancing.

Flakes land like feathers,
ridge down my back
like the comb of a fighting dragon.

God has issued his decree—
from January on,
we are all to be hermits.

This winter, my Irish cousins
tell me of the misery
of the wolves of Cuan Wood:
so bent with cold they cannot rest;

the eagles of Glen Rye
are breaking icicles
from the bitter winds
with their deadly beaks.

Full lakes are frozen seas;
tiny meres are full lakes;

horses spin
on these iron fields
like priests with brandy;

fishes plough the gray waves
just to keep warm.

Snow mounts higher
than the mountain.

Bells are frozen in the black chapel.
The shield hangs idle on the warrior's shoulder.

A WORD TO THE MEN

Irish, by Laoiseach Mac an Bhaird, sixteenth century

O you that follow English ways,
who cut your curling hair,

your horse does not gallop
the same proud acres
as the good son of Donnchadh.

If you truly were his cousins,
you would not be so quick

to trade your rebel locks
for the tonsure of a loveless priest.

That wild shock of yellow hair
is a rooster's comb
to the son of Donnchadh.

He doesn't care for breeches,
for doublet or for hose,

or a gentlemen's rapier
that could not kill a fly.

For myself, I know a hero
—his name is Eoghan Ban.

He gives no time to delicate ruffs,
gold-lined cloaks, or satin scarves.

A hut of rough wattles,
to Eoghan Ban,

makes a sweeter nest
than the lonely castle.

He prefers to lie on rushes
than a courtier's feather bed

to meet a troop of horses
at the mouth of a pass,
to raise his fists for honor,

to seek hard contest with these foreigners.

These are meat and ale
of the son of Donnchadh.

You have nothing on him,
our champion of the lanes.

With every falling lock,

you set your foot
on the mounting block,

O you who follow English ways.

LAMENT FOR THE FOUR MACDONALDS

Scottish-Irish, by Cathal MacMhuirich, 1636

Bitter our hearts
now the brave heroes
of the Race of Conn are dead.

We won't last long
without them.

Unparalleled their gifts to poets;
unstinting with a cloak, horse or golden cup;
it's unsettling to be abandoned
with them under the gray clay.

Since soil has concealed them, all has changed:
a sorrow-deluge claiming the land.
Our herds do not increase,
the woods are bare-crested,
and the branching bough
does not bend with ripe fruit.

If you know the language
you can hear the lament;
mountain stream, and wailing bird
and catchless nets from the lake.

Dry weather is a fable, a rumor.
Waves gnaw the peaks of hills,
our corn and hay
are pulped by storms.

This grief has made a crow of me,
and not myself alone.
The state of education is easy to see
in the funeral dress of the poets.

It's over.

When men do speak, their words are spiked
with gloom and wrath.
We no longer can hear the cuckoo's song,
the rivers no longer are silver with fish.

And the wind is a brute,
thrashing down the heather.

FIONN'S MIGRATIONS

of the Irish folk-hero Fionn mac Cumhaill

> He was a King, a seer and a poet. He was a lord with a manifold
> and great train. He was our magician, our knowledgeable one,
> our soothsayer. All that he did was sweet with him. And, however
> you deem my testimony excessive, I state by the King above me,
> Fionn was three times better than all I say.
>
> *–Saint Patrick*

Fionn as a pup.
First among the bulrushes
and the branchy wood,
jaw raised for the cold clear tappings

of rain that sloughed
from leaf to leaf.
Fionn, hoof-foot on the tough
brown paths of the forest.

Fionn alone.

That boy who was raised
in wild, green acres
under the blue tent of the sky.

His father Cumhaill had been slain
by men jealous for his place;
captain of the Fianna of Ireland.
Fianna—the warrior elite.

Their hair braided,
their skulls alive with poetry,
their speech like scarlet berries.

The Fianna—Cumhaill was their Rooster,
his speech like honeycomb;
first to take the shield-wall;
and a warm hand on the shoulder.

But to live like that
is to attract attention;
to feel the jealous glance of other men;
to hear their mutters in the mead-hall.

One morning Cumhaill's enemies caught him
off his guard
and took him, and gutted him.

When his father was gutted
Fionn's mother—Muirne of the dark-river hair—
knew they would come for the child.

So Fionn was kept secret,
his den low-slung.
His harbor far down in the quiet
gut of the forest,

cheek-close to the caw, croak, whistle
and chirp of the forest.

They owned nothing
they could not shift in an hour.

• • •

Fionn, alone.
Became a great listener,
curled in the yellow gaze
of lonely sunshine,
ear bent to the thousand-voiced wind.

Fionn spoke bird:
rival to the reed-croak of the jackdaw,
his raw speech warbled
its twigged praise.

Rough-skinned from thickets, and sharp tufts of nettle,
knees blue from long hours
standing in water,
watching the otter.

A lover of briar
and the quiet croft,
of low-shaken apple trees
and the sap of the alder.

His amiable gaze would settle
on whatever beast made it through
the rough hedge of his walls.

The solemn horse,
the milk-rich cow,
the spider on the leaf,
the lightning-swift fly.

Strange bliss for the boy was his loneliness.

● ● ●

How to make a hero?

The women-druids
made sure to give their boy-charge
news of his enemies:

the four sons of Morna,
the ones who dragged Fionn's father into hell:

of Conan Mael,
tough as a badger and bald as a crow;
bearded as a boar, who could find an insult
where another could not find a stammer.

Who never saw a door without the urge
to kick it open,
who never saw a face and thought it not his duty
to strike it.

And Conan Mael was rarely without the savage Art Og,
and rough Mac Morna,
those double terror bringers.

These untamable Connachtmen,
with no mind for safety,
as terrible and strange as their own land.

The nurses of Fionn made a quill of their vocation:
and dripped revenge like ink
on the blank page of their lad.

• • •

Fionn grew.
His shape leapt toward manhood.

He lit the yellow candle
on his deep pool of thought.
Taking note of his seasons, his guardians
threw their oracle bones.

They measured the shadows,
discussed the cloud-shapes, the flight of a swift.

• • •

Around that time, one morning,
tromping through the woods

came the high trill of youth;
a band of poets from the Galtees.

These junior-bards were returning home,
clucking with rhyme and tricks of learning.

Young Fionn fell in with them, and went adventuring
with his keepers' approval—
on the move, less easy to trace.
Never before had Fionn been shoulder-thick
in the company of other boys:

a gabble loose with the crack,
with tales of lust and courage—
with legends of young bravos wandering.

Their boots and cloaks
and the high-clatter of their speech
was heady beer to the forest boy.

At night beside a poacher's fire
his head rested on rowan roots.
He felt the world lope toward him.

But it would never be his way
to run too long with packs.

● ● ●

Early morning their path was crossed
by something demon-dark;

a Leinsterman, Fiacuil Mac Cona, the great robber,
a man at war against the world.

His darkness fell upon them:
his blade fell to carving.
He hurled them from this world,

Only Fionn remained,
big with rage; teeth snarled like a dog's,
fists raised against blade.

"What name do you go by?" roared Fiacuil,
and Fionn replied,
"Son of Cumhaill, Son of Baiscne."

At this, the murderer halted;
a blackthorn club no more,

but a weeping man in the presence
of the son of his great captain.

A man at war with the world
that took his leader.

Since the Clann-Baiscne was broken
he had taken to the hard wilds,
bedded down in a grim marsh.

He swooped the boy onto his shoulders
and his great dark horse, making snorts and jumps,
and took him to the burrow of his home.

And that was how young Fionn
acquired his next instructor.

• • •

A genius of weapons, Fiacuil
gave the boy instruction:
how to chop and slice; to be nimble under fire,
how to practice patience.

His great spear was Fiacuil's deepest pride,
with thirty rivets of Arab gold in its socket
—beautiful when idle, wrapped up and tied down
but wild and murderous when it came to life.

Fionn's tutoring was always more than human:
the dank marsh, with its treacherous secrets

gurgled webbed advice to his young ear;
a watery guide, not the firm plain of earth.

The robber spoke of coiling weeds,
of tentacle-roots under the brown waters,
of thin, snaky bindings that would trap any diver.

"Learn to understand what is underneath water,"
counseled Fiacuil,
"and always swim
with a knife between your teeth."

In time once more Fionn took his leave
of swamp and teacher.

Like a crane upon the mud flats
whose frame has settled for a while,
he felt the time of his departure.

He felt that world lurch toward him.

• • •

Fionn abroad.

To shoulder loneliness,
this would always be his way.

When all is said, whatever came to Fionn
also went from him,
and happiness, as people think of it,
was never his for long.

No half-blind tramp was he:
his eyes were sharp and strong.

From far off he could see
the hare crouching in new corn,

the trout suspended on gray shale,
the shadow-birds under the oak's bough.

His eye was a sharp optic,
slicing the atom, dappling the air.
Hour by hour, it was a world
in full disclosure.

• • •

Time passes
while drinking water from icy rivers.
Under fast gray skies,
the ground runs beneath our feet.

Grown into proper shape,
Fionn roamed and changed:
his wanderings took him
down highways and to travelers' camps;

he learned laughing among strangers,
and the taste of women;
but for Fionn peace was in the wild,
and he was never sad to bed by fawn and under birch.

• • •

O world of myriad desires:
Fionn had them too.

He had the lasting one:
the search for wisdom.

He took himself to the
bank of the River Boyne.

And there it was he met his second solitary—
the hermit Finegas, a poet-man;
brilliant, wise, and kind.

After years of incubation,
all Fionn's questions hatched at once,
and ran about:

"Why do you live by flowing water?"

"Because a poem is a kind of revealing,
and at the bank of running water
the poem is revealed to us."

"How long have you been here?"

"Seven years," said the man.

"A long time," whispered Fionn.

"I would settle twice the distance
for a good poem," smiled Finegas.

"Have you caught good poems?"

"What I was ready for has found me:

you can't reach for more than that—
our readiness is our limit."

Fionn ate it up.

"Would the poems have been more great
by the majestic Shannon, or the Liffey?"

"They are good rivers too,
of which you speak,
and they belong to their good gods."

The elder man leaned forward.
"A man of foresight did predict

that I would catch the Salmon of Knowledge
in the Boyne waters.

This would, in turn,
give me all knowledge."

"What would you do with it?"

"That's a question with horns, lad.
What would you do?"

"I would make a poem," cried Fionn.

"I think," spoke Finegas,
"I think that is what would happen."

● ● ●

Fionn made himself a pupil.

He gave himself fully
to the service of his master's hut:
he carried water and kept the fire;
he cut dry rushes for the floor.

He was taught the rules of meter,
the cunning scope of words,
and the high calling
for a clean, brave mind.

This Finegas was as a god to Fionn.

In his patience and unstinting kindness,
his skill as a teacher,
and most of all as the ordained eater
of the Salmon of Knowledge.

Fionn was at the feet of an Old One,
and he loved him.

Fionn's questions continued to leap
from the green waves of his thinking:

"How does the salmon get
wisdom into his flesh?"

"Not hard to answer," told Finegas.

"Overhanging a secret pool
there is a hazel bush.

Its ripe seeds drop from bush to pool,
and the salmon eats them."

Flushed, the boy spoke:

"Could we not just track the sacred hazel,
and eat them ourselves?"

"Such a bush could be discovered only
by eating the seeds;

those very seeds that can only be found
by eating the salmon."

Fionn writhed, then wrestled out his patience.
They must wait for the salmon.

● ● ●

One day Finegas came to where Fionn sat,
a basket on his arm
both spring and winter in his expression.

"What is the matter, master?" enquired Fionn.
"Look in the basket, lad," replied Finegas.

Fionn gazed into the basket.
"Ah, a salmon."

Sighed Finegas, "It is the Salmon.
I wish you to roast it for me,
as I take a short walk to gather myself."

Fionn cooked as never before.
Smoked on a wooden platter,

the fish nestled between green leaves,
a delirium of scent.

Finegas returned for his high moment.
Eyes scanned his student tenderly.

"Did you not take a bit for yourself?" he asked.
"I left so you might eat the fish, if so compelled."

The boy spoke, proud and wounded.
"Why would I take another man's fish?"

"Youth rides the red horse of desire," spoke the poet,
"and even a taste constitutes its eating."

At this Fionn chuckled.
"By chance, I might have got the merest flavor;

for a great blister arose onto the skin,
not suitable to my chef's eye,

not for your great meal and all.
So I pressed it down with my thumb,

and I placed that thumb in the cave of my mouth,
to cool the smart."

The old man winced, just a little.
"My love, tell me your name?"

"My name is Deimne, as I have said before."
"Your name is not Deimne, it is Fionn."

Fionn was startled, knocked off his perch.

"How could you know this without
tasting the Salmon?" he asked.

"In that prediction of my catching the Salmon,
it was said that it would be eaten by Fionn, Son of Cumhaill and Baiscne."

Tears pricked the eyes of the young hero.
"You shall have half this fish with me, here and now!"

The bard trembled and stood back.
"No bone, no skin, no flesh shall I eat.

This feast is yours; as I leave libation
to the mossy gods of the Underworld
and the forces of the Air."

Fionn sat and ate the Salmon of Knowledge,
his master watching in the half-light.

When it was done, a great tranquility
swept into the frame of Finegas.

"It was quite a battle with that fish," he spoke.
"Did it give good account for its life?"

"It did, but that is not the battle I speak of."

The two men cleaned up and made fire,
drank tea, and sat out under a hundred thousand stars.

• • •

Fionn for destiny.

With the eating of the Salmon,
his time with the flowing water and Finegas
was up.

His father's reckoning was upon him.

He put weight to his thigh
and headed toward the heart of old Ireland,
Tara of the Kings.

Sailing like Jason,
toward who knows what.

It was Samhain.

The land combed red and bronze-gold;
air sharp with frost
the crunch of leaf-meal
under your foot.

Time of autumn beef and red ale,
the silver canopy of the rain,

a thick cloak with a bronze clasp,
a fire that holds embers all night.

Time for the bard to tune his harp,
for spitted ox, a keg,
blue fingers as kindling is gathered,
a friendly hound, a bed.

Samhain is the name of the season,
the great un-tethering of boundaries
between living and dead,
the chariot-swift faery,
and the boundless denizens of night.

And let me tell you of Tara.

The high king's palace,
replete with fortification,
and then another, enclosing
four minor palaces,
presided by the four provincial kings.

There was the mighty feasting hall,
and holding all,
the sacred tump itself,
the vast green hill that
gripped the outer ramparts.

Issuing from this axis-mundi were four roads:
north, south, east, west,
directioned to the four quadrants of Erin.

A dragoned spiral,
white-boned with ancestry,
rough-mudded with spell.

The city was bright.
Roofs painted with the colors of a bird,
so they appeared as feathered wings.

The palaces were sturdy with ancient red oak,
polished and worn,
pillars of burnished bronze.

Tara was an elegant fist,
gathering in the gold of the dying sun,

sweeping up the gray teeth of the sea,
the red heaven of soil and branch.

It was a jubilation.

• • •

As Fionn entered,
the feasting of Samhain was soon to commence,
and all men found themselves neighbors and allies.

The wicks were lit,
noble and consort drank of the full glass,
wolfhounds were a-bliss with scraps.

And there, on the raised dais
which commanded the great hall
were the men who had killed Fionn's father,
flushed with wine and praise.

The High King, the Ard-Ri,
Conn of the Hundred Battles,
peered through the blue smoke
and saw that this guest had no seat.

When no one knew his name,
Conn took the horn of state
and spoke out over the humming room.

"Gentleman, I wish to toast
your health and welcome you to Tara.
But first I must ask;
what is your name?"

The man stepped into clear view.
Broad as an ox, long-limbed,
great-shouldered;
his face unbearded, his curls a torrent.

Conn handed him the horn to speak.

"I am Fionn, the son of Cumhaill, the son of Baiscne."

The room was first lightning-struck;
then it smoldered, grievous with shock.

Fionn gave the strong eye
to the twinkling countenance of Goll.
But no movement to sword, no shout of disquiet.

Good Conn spoke up:
"You are the son of a friend.
Please, sit amongst us."

He ushered Fionn to a seat
at the right hand
of his own son Art.

• • •

Despite the shockwave of Fionn's arrival,
its bold and prophetic aura,
another drama slouched on the hall that night.

For the last nine Samhains,
a foe from the Otherworld, Aillen mac Midna,
had taken penalty from Tara.

A dark Grendel,
a brute-demon.

Each year on this date
Aillen would enter this world,
swinging black fists into damage.

Though the city still stood, many died.

Rumor insisted it revenge
for some rough voyaging into the Land of Sidhe
Conn had undertaken as a youth.

When Conn spoke to the bold assembly
as to who would take
the night watch outside the hall,

no tongue was moved to eloquence,
no warrior-kit was gathered,
no lingering stroke of a lover's hair,
no knee bent for the blessing of a king.

These burning bushes of violence,
these dark-bruised crows of battle,
took to nibbling their fingernails,
or enquiring of the sleeping accommodations.

Piss dribbled
from the top tables,
Even Goll's shameless cheek
had lost some of its color.

But Fionn alone.

The solitary stood,
alive to possibility:
"What will be given to he
who undertakes this defense?"

Spoke Conn:

"All that can be rightly asked
will be royally bestowed,
with the sureties of the Irish Kings
and Red Cith with his magicians."

"I will take up the defense,"
said the fair one.

• • •

It is a long walk through the fortifications,
then the great, outer wall,
and onto the wide plain of Tara.

Long enough to sober a man.

No one but the mad
were abroad on a night like this.
Only those sickened by the moon,
or strutting the left-magic-path.

As Fionn turned back to survey,
the jutting ramparts blotted
the lanterns of the city, and blocked out entirely
all noise of celebration.

Ah, to be far from the feast.

Turf underneath foot.
Coal-night overhead.
Darkness.
Wind.

He gave himself to gazing,
this man who caught the hundred moods of night,
who saw dappled light
where we see a black sheet.

• • •

A man is coming, Fionn thought.
An ally:
his walk is open.

Slipping back into his life,
stalked the good robber, Fiacuil.

"Ah, great pulse of mine," breathed Fionn,
"are you not a-fear to be out
on this plain?"

"True, true," spoke Fiacuil,
"and when business is finished,
off I will trot.

But firstly, young friend, I must tell you
that no simple attack will work in this fight.
This beast brings music and fire.

First, the music sedates with its sweet, low tune.
And when all slumber,
its breath-fire torches all.

But I can help with this."

"And what would be payment?" mused Fionn.

"A mere third of your earnings, my lad;
and a seat at your council, as well."

"I grant that, bold friend," said Fionn,
"now, what is your plan?"

And Fiacuil produced his spear—
the venom-rich Birgha,
with its thirty rivets of Arabian gold,
and its head wrapped in a blanket.

"It is the being's own spear,
taken from the land of the Sidhe by your father.

When it comes, as it soon will,
unwrap the spear
and bend your face to the head.

Its stink,
its heat,
its acrid wisps
will keep you from sleep.

Take it,
fear it,
release the eerie
right back to its owner."

The package given,
Fiacuil made off, for surely now
the darkness was darker
than when conversation began.

• • •

It was the moon that announced,

that started gleaming strangely;
a percolation of light
threading through low cloud.

Fionn heard the bold step.

It was not a thing he saw,
but a spirit-kingdom on the move.
A rattled-atmosphere,
snaked and hoofed,
sonorous with terror-gloom.

Just one being,
but a multitude within.

Not a presence to linger with,
not even in description.

But the sweetness of the music!

It was an otherly thrill,
gamboling the long grasses;
a perfume that clouded over
the firm plain of Tara.

It entered your bone-house,
and slumbered your heart.

Fionn removed his spear's hood
and took a deep snuffle
of the wretch-heavy air
around the shapely iron.

Its point sizzled, eager for fulfillment,
it strained to be thrust in his mighty paw.

In its stink-aura,
sleep could not claim residence.

The beast, no wiser, aimed a blue fire
at the City of Kings,
sharp as a thunderbolt.

But with an old cunning,

Fionn spread the mantle, caught the flame,
and hurled it into the soil.
That slope they still call the Glen of the Mantle
and the Ard of Fire.

When a second flaming went the way of the first,
even a god of the Sidhe knew panic.

Aillen turned his face then, toward the blue night,
filled with the sudden intention
to hoof back to his own kingdom.

Fionn pursued
and released the Birgha—

swiftly that deadly black finger
was reunited with its master.

• • •

Dawn was breaking
a gold-reddened sunrise
as Fionn made the walk
into the Hall of Champions.

All leaned forward.

One arm aloft,
swung by a bundle of hair,
like a trophy won at the fair,
Fionn held the precious head of Aillen.

The Ard-Ri raised grateful voice:
"What is your demand?"

"Only a thing of deep rightness,"
said the night-watchman,
"the command of the Fianna of Ireland."

Conn turned to Goll Mor,
chief man of the warriors.

"Here are the turns in your road.
Let me clearly describe them:
either leave Ireland today and forever,

or place your hand and service
into the keep of this young champion."

Goll did not swerve at the challenge,
and spoke from the full quiver of his sincerity:
"Here is my hand."

In the bronzed light, Goll's eyes twinkled
at the sight

of this stern young solitary
absorbing his submission.

This is just a little
of what makes a champion.

LAMENT FOR REILLY

Irish, traditional folk song

As I walked the strand one fine evening,
whom did I see but my fair-haired Reilly?

His cheeks were flushed and his brown hair all curly
and I felt that his death was galloping through me.

My God, Reilly, were you not the king's son-in-law,
meant to be dressed in the finest gold cloth?

With bright white curtains around where you lay,
and a graceful lady combing your hair?

The shipwright who made the boat for your journey,
may his two hands crumble like old brown cork.

May the leaking plank in the hull of that boat
be burnt alive in a fire.

May the cold sea that surged through the hole in that plank
be jailed, found guilty, and hanged.

May the priest who prayed on the deck, and failed,
go to no heaven.

If I had been out that night with my nets all ready,
by God, Reilly, I would have saved you.

You looked so grand on your white horse last summer,
sounding your horn, your hounds by your side.

God made me alone so young; I hear them
repeating that Reilly is dead, my Reilly is dead again.

You should have heard their voices that night;
so excited to know there would be

not a wedding, but a wake;
and a brand new widow.

THE TURN IN THE ROAD

Welsh, from traditional verse, seventeenth century

Past forty,
a man can carry

the flush
of a tree in leaf,

or shoulder a
quiver of speech.

He can laugh quietly
over his scars.

But the sound of
that vault being opened

lets the
crow settle

on the soft acres
of his face.

THE BLACK-HAIRED LAD

Scottish-Gaelic, traditional folk song, before 1776

I'll not climb the brae, or walk on the moor.
My voice is wrecked, no song left in me;
I'll not sleep an hour Monday till Sunday
while the black-haired lad comes to mind.

I grieve I'm not with the black-haired lad
on the brow of a hill under rainstorms, tucked
away in a hollow or safe secret place;
and I'll not take a graybeard
while he comes to mind.

I would kneel and drink the health of the black-haired lad
from the dark water of the moor
as gladly as wine;
though many men come to woo me,
I'll not take a graybeard while he comes to mind.

A generous man, ungrudging he is;
a lover of girls, and a drinker of wine.
Manly and hard-striking, a hunter on the moors;
and I'll not take a graybeard while he comes to mind.

My handsome love!—though all think him reckless,
I would marry him without consent of my kin.
And I will roam through dells and wild places
and I'll not take a graybeard
while the black-haired lad comes to mind.

ARRAN

Irish, author unknown, twelfth century

Arran of the plentiful stag, where the sea
splashes its shoulder;
island where warriors are fed;
ridge where blue spears are reddened.

Clear water courses the streams;
nuts abundant upon brown oaks.
And all the heath in autumn
is mellow with blueberry.

In spring, the lichen on rocks is purple;
fawns gambol, trout leap,
stags drift unwary,
like unmoored boats
amongst the dark blackthorn.

This is a tale you may trust:
the swine are fat in that land;
around its white cliffs
seagulls angle and croon,
Arran of the plentiful stag.

BLODEUEDD OF THE OWL-FACE

Welsh, author unknown

They all knew Llew was handsome.

Llew Llaw Gyffes:
a laughing boy, stag-proud:
                    wheat-blond, a lively wit
                              but gracious to all.
A catch.

Surely one parade of the market square,
one giddy night of dancing
would capture him a bride?

But no.

Years before, his own mother
had pointed her calm finger in his direction

and swore that he would never take a wife
from any race on this earth.

Oh, he could rut till he was giddy,
grow hair-backed and barking in the May Day rituals,
—no deeper union would be his.

He would be never truly rooted to a woman.

With her unmotherly hex,
she thinned his lovemaking,

trimmed the banks of his wildflowers
to a stubble,
drained his forest pool of all its gloaming fishes.

Bait would drag his shallows and no more.

Off you go, lover-man.

• • •

Llew's uncle, Gwydion, was a witch of repute.
He observed this crippling with a keen eye.

Saw his nephew grow thinner
with each amorous clamber,

a waning not suited to his years.

Vast Gwydion resolved to help.

With another cunning man, Math,
he looked hard for a crack
                    in the old bitch's casting.

"On this earth?" they asked each other;
"What if she was not from this earth?"

With their night intelligence
they packed provisions for a quest—a hunter's kit—
                    and made for the black hills.

Shuddering in gale, salmon-pinked by sun,
they scooped up flowers of the oak, the golden broom,
                    and the sweet meadow-lace.

Gathered tumps of wild blossoms,
and heaped them like a woman's curves,
                    until a body was arrayed on the sweet grasses:

a fume-tangle of scent,
of delicate buds and foliaged beauty.

Then they muttered with their stubbled jaws,
and cast arcs of potion liberally over

        the sex, the heart, the brain of this leafy thing.

This great ship of flora,
wet-rooted in the underswing of earth,

        drawn up into collaboration with freezing blue stars.

Proper magic.

Wild geese in the smoky air
peered down at the changeling,

        a shape alive—shifting in invisible gusts;

rootsy hips, mooned face,

        scalding the wetling grasses.

It was two who went up.
It was three that came down from the hills.

• • •

They named her Blodeuedd—"Flowers."
Her eerie beauty caught Llew agape.

        One glance at her threshold

and he threw all his affections
into the pen of love's wild horses.

Soon, they married—
Bloudeuedd and Llew—

        that elemental woman and the lad of the valleys.

One morning some time later,
whilst Llew was abroad with Math,

        Blodeuedd was roused by a horn outside the castle.

From her window she saw in the morning fog,
a stag burst from the thicket;

then foam-jawed hounds
and behind them huntsmen—

a line of pursuers, ancient and stylish.

That apparition of men
was like a bell ringing inside her;
                    like a scene from a tapestry.

Their leader? Gronw, lord of Penllyn.
The flower maiden catches just a second
                    of his dark shape cantering by,
but it is enough.

Maybe some copsy scent clung to the Hunter-Lord,
maybe he smelt of her home, of earth.
                    He was a deep music to her green inner form.

That evening the men are invited to supper
and to lodge in the castle.

Thatched torches are lit in the stone corridors,
mead sweetens the salt from the chops,
                    the gallery swells with minstrels.

In the candled gloom, love and its transgressions
            rise up between Blodeuedd and Gronw.

It is one thing to feel, quite another to act.
Still, they do.

Her boy-husband might be riding his horse
off the very edge of the world
                    for all she knew, or cared.

In the nights they spent together, their trysting
grew bolder, requiring broader ground.

"How do we rid ourselves of Llew?" mutters the suitor, sourly.

"He is riddled with enchantments" she said;
"There must be a science to his dying
                         that I shall make my business to gather."

Gronw nods, unblinking.

• • •

When Llew returns, his wife is remote—
swathed in a distance all to herself.
The merry stories of his journey fall sour between them.

Groping into the air, panicked,
he asks about her silence: Is she sick?

She gathered her fiction:
"Not sick, beloved, but worried.
                         Anxious that one day you may die
                                   and I would have to live on."

Relieved at her concern, he speaks with confidence,

"Ah, well if that is all, I have good news.
           The killing of me would not be an easy thing—
                         the murderer would need information
only the gods could supply."

Blodeuedd leaned in now, flushed.
"Ah such good news! Please,
                  put my mind at rest, tell me of its nature,

so I can put such crow-aches from my heart."

He reveals: "Certainly.

I can only be butchered by the tip of a spear
that has taken a year to create,

and the forging of such a spear can only be
on the morning hours of a Sunday,
                              when all are worshipping.

I cannot be killed in a house or outside a house.
Not on horseback or on foot.

The only way it could happen is this:
a bath would be made upon a riverbank,
    and roofed with thatch.
A goat would be produced and tethered by the tub.

If I placed one foot on the goat, and one on the rim of the bath,
and if that spear was thrown,
                    then, and only then, could I be slain."

His wife absorbed the facts,
nestled them in her breast,
steadied the information,
                    and got message to Gronw.

With his fierce face and skilled hand
he slipped to the forge in the praying times of each Sunday
                              and got to work.

Outside of chapel's godly care,
he plied his terrible attentions,
                    blistered his paws,
                        was grunt-back-bent over the hot iron.

It took one year, but Gronw made the spear.
The Flowered Wife did not forget him,
did not veer from the plan.

Blodeuedd spoke up to Llew.
"Sweetheart. Indulge me.
                I still am fearful of your death.

Would you not consider
                creating the very scene that you described?
                                The bath, the goat?

So that I can see just how unlikely it would be
that such forces would align.

In the seeing of it somehow I believe
                my fear would set me free."

Lacking the foresight of age,
Llew agreed to the request,
                eagerly producing the materials for his own ambush.

Blodeuedd sent word to Gronw the dark.

She prepared the bath on the riverbank,
made sure the water was warm, and scented with sweet herbs.
                Llew sloshed about, then settled in his wife's attention.

She produced a rugged brown goat.
                "Now darling—could you just rise and show me
                                how you would balance on the goat and the tub?"

Naked, the trusting husband rose,
dripping and shivering in cold Welsh air,
                gingerly balancing on the edge of the tub,
                                placing one foot on the goat's curved back.

When his wobbling settled, when he was clearly in place,
Blodeuedd let out the death-shriek she had harbored so long,

and from the bleak copse emerged Gronw.

With the strength of his father, and his father's father,
   he hurled the spear straight at the trembling form of Llew.

Such was the force that when it hit
  Llew—in the side of his body—

the shaft broke off and the head of the spear
  stayed embedded in the wound.

Screaming, stricken, rough with blood,
  Llew spasmed into eagle-shape, a man no more
    and, with head of the spear still gutted-fast, flew from sight.

● ● ●

Time passes.
Cold news of the betrayal reaches Gwydion and Math,

the Frankensteins to this floral deceiver.

Low with worry,
Gwydion stalks the land, the seaports,
    the humped and rutted tracks of farmers,

looking for a hint of where the bird-man has gone.
Around his raw knuckles he wraps prayer-words
    that this boy still lives.

Many would have given up.

One day in early winter, he comes to a farm.
Frost has stiffened his cloak,
    aches abide in his bone-house.

Talking to the swineherd about anything unusual
in the local weather, movement of animals,
    the magics of the settlement.

The farm boy has one thought only:
of a sow that trots briskly when the sty is opened

across the frozen soil and out into the forest,

never followed by others; always
                returning drowsy and content.

A thin lead, indeed, but perhaps enough.

Enough for Gwydion to take a night's rest at the place.
              At dawn he strolls in cold gold light along the sow's trail.

Upstream, he follows, then across scattered fields,
             farther over hills to a quiet valley.

The sow waddles
             to a fat trunked oak, its northern flank moss-thick.

In the muddied roots the beast starts to snuffle
             and over the minutes that follow, a shower of ripe flesh

begins to fall from the higher branches,
                to the grunting pleasure of the sow.

Glancing up, at the very top of the tree, the uncle
             spies an eagle, loosening a treasure of maggoted meat
                  to its slobbering ally at the base.

Gwydion knew the inner-shape of that bird.
So he began to sing:

"Between two lakes an old oak grows,
sheltered from cold wind that blows
I know I do not tell a lie—
my nephew Llew rests there on high."

Cocking his head, the eagle
dropped from the high branches to the middle.

"There is an oak on an upland plain,
not scorched by sun, or wet with rain;
may his hardships soon be o'er
and Llew restored to us once more."

Again the eagle dropped down now
to the lowest branches.

For the final time, Gwydion sang:

"Grows an oak upon a steep
where a lord his home does keep;
if I do not speak falsely,
Llew will come on to my knee."

The eagle alighted onto Gwydion's knee.

With a small cut of rowan branch,
the enchanter stroked the back of the eagle's head,
                         shape-lurching from bird back into Llew,

scrappily awake, deep flustered,
             naked and blue-skinned on the winter turf.

Crumpled, and shrunk, not quite alive.
Just an imprint of his former self.

Wrapping him in his cloak, Gwydion shouldered
as best he could the shrunken man,

his bird-voice adrift between species.

At the chambers of Math, the greatest of physicians
the born-again Llew is attended from all sides.

He raged, sweat-shimmered through blue night,
slammed his forelock on the buttress of death;

floundered through shape again and again.
Sometimes tufted, sometimes a bone-cairn.

Only gradually, like the wheeling seasons, buds of green
        appeared through the ice-sheets of his illness.

• • •

They all knew Llew was handsome.
But now they'd find that he was deadly.

Gronw, when he heard of this return,
shat hot liquid, a-quake with fear
                        for what was coming.

He sends over parley of silver, and gold,
but he finds deaf ears.

Llew demands meeting by the very spot
where the harpoon was thrown.

Black Gronw became Gronw of the Grovel
as he begs for a stone to be placed between

the two men, for he knows the man means to hurl his spear.

When Llew agrees, Gronw produces nothing less
than a granite block
                higher than a man between them.

No matter.

It was an ancient spear, whetted with cave magic,
        it split the rock like summer butter,
                and skewered the lord fast to the dark pitch
                        of soil.

For Gronw, no swift ending.

It was Gwydion who tracked his creature down,
        the Woman of the Flowers.

In a place far from villages,
        surrounded by maidens,
who wailed through the drizzle mist

when the death-magus slowly cantered toward them,
        his long fingers hexing their mistress.

As one, they moved backward,
paying no mind to the ancient lake behind them.

The hooves of their steeds sliding mad
                on the guttered banks

as the green-lipped waters
rose and took them down
under the singing roof of wave.

Only Blodeuedd stood still, her horse jaded
                by the magnetism of the wizard.

"Slaying," spoke Gwydion, "is not my business with you.
But some other hurt I will provoke.

Oh, I release you from this human form, Blodeuedd.

You will be a bird. But a bird that will not
                feel sun caught in its feathers.

Ebony wanderer, moon-faced, trouble-hunted by all other birds.
An owl you will be.
This is your difficult trail, faithless one."

But what had she been faithless to?
        Did anyone ask what gods she followed?

Surely this harm falls at her creator's hand too.

These thoughts ride alongside.

On the back of her head, he tapped once with his wand

and her face, for a second,
                        was ablaze again with flowers.

Her eyes rolled back in their foliaged pits,
                with an eerie goodness, a body lit from inside.

Then taking the luna-round shape of the gloaming bird,

the owl thrust out,
        took wing and was gone,

gone beyond,
        deep into the wet flank of the woods.

THE YARROW CHARM

Scottish-Gaelic, traditional folk charm

I kneel and pluck
the smooth yarrow

to spell-make,
to intrigue the stars to me.

Give elegance to my figure.
Subtract a little from the hips.

May my voice carry cheer,
like the yellowed sun,

may my lips be succulent, full and red,
like the juice of strawberries.

I shall be an island
in the blue-black waves,

a wooded hill on the land,
a sturdy ash staff when my heart is weak.

And just to be clear:

I shall wound every man,
but no man shall wound me.

CROOKED STICK

Welsh, attributed to Llywarch Hen, ninth century

Crooked stick, it is autumn, bracken red;
stubble of fields pale yellow.

Crooked stick, it is winter; men boisterous
over their beer.

Crooked stick, it is spring; cuckoos brown;
warming light at evening meal.

Crooked stick, it is summer, red furrow and corn curly;
I am shapeless and old on my couch.

The wind drives the leaf; that's its fate.
White is the snow at the edge of the woods.

Crooked stick, I'm sorrowed at your shape,
irritable and unsteady.

Who I loved in boyhood, I now hate:
a girl, a stranger, a gray horse.

MIDHIR'S INVITATION TO THE FAIR LAND

Irish, author unknown, ninth century

Fair woman, will you go with me to the high land
where sweet music is? There your hair is like the primrose
and people stroll with snow-white skin.

In the high land, there is neither *yours* nor *mine*.
The women's teeth are white; the men's eyes are black and clear.

Every cheek is the pink of foxglove.

The meadows of Ireland are fair to see—
but they are like a desert when you have seen the high land;

Irish ale is fine to drink—but in the high land
the wine they serve will turn your head into a cloud.

In the place I speak of, the young do not die before their time;
they serve the old ones, who are wise
and shield the young in turn.

Sweet streams flow always through the fair land
and the minds of the people are clear

as skin with no blemish,
as a child's face in the virgin morning.

When we walk together there, you will see
these men and ladies,

you will see them on all sides, tall and fair and kind.
But they will not see us.

For Adam's transgression is a dark cloak around us,
and it means we cannot be seen, or counted among them.

WISE MORNING

Welsh, traditional verse, seventeenth century

It is a strange cheer
to take to the storm,

to gird my rain-kit,
to light the wick,

and broach the shores
of the Menai.

But I do,
as my father did.

I set to my
melancholy penance.

The herring drift happy
under the wild ink's spuming,

this granary
for salt-horses,

this crab-thick black,
that shudders under my lantern.

A bleak wine
that brims up the lip of the sand.

A thousand ships of sorrow
drift

by the whales' dark fields.
My boat hugs the shore

as the sea has its way.

Each dawn a new scene
at the shores of Menai,

the wind like a breeze over barley,
the sea playful,

like a foal with its mother,

as the sun bakes the stones
of the walls of Carnarvon.

Let the morning
be wiser than the evening.

THE HORNED WOMEN

Irish, author unknown

The heavy house in the storm
is resting.
It values girth over migration;

robust with creaking,
it stays its compass,
resists invasion from the gale-ing heave.

Sullen and slumbered in the epileptic rain.

Above, Orion lopes in his black jungle,

with his triple-starred belt, his hunter charms;
fast-moving over the weather, the house, the people.

But this is not his story.

Below, children are curled pink in blankets,
servants doze with their thin hounds
by the twinkling peat.

Only the Big Woman of the house is awake,
working by candle
nailed fast to her evening task, the carding of wool.

She is deep in the hut of herself.

Something haunches through sleet outside
to the old door,
and sets up a clamor,

part voice and part knock;
brick-fisted and gallop-jawed;

"Open! Open!"

Big Woman calls, "Who is there?"
Comes grizzled croak, tindered with soot;
"I am the Witch of the One Horn."

Suspecting a villager's trick,
the mistress groans open the oak,
and the weird being comes in,
parading a pair of wool carders in her left hand,

and, truly, a horn, a bone-white horn
from her forehead's crown,
as if still in growth.

She slow-hoofs to the hearthside and starts carding the wool,
granite-knuckled but finger-nimble.

Once more a something batters the door;
another voice, silvered with water;
"I am the Witch of the Two Horns."

An elegant wraith enters,
with a wheel for spinning, a hand sparrow-quick for the task,
and a double white horn aglow from her skull.

That night through the juddering dark,
twelve women in all glide in,
the last with twelve horns jutting
her brow, ornate and terrible,

like the jaw of an Irish shark,
a glinting underworld crown.

Saying nothing to the Big Woman,
they settle to their spinning
and ply their family conversation

with a moon-cold language,
like lumps of ice from a frozen lake,
or words gathered from underneath a stone.

That keening drains the mistress of the house,
renders her silent, giddy, and weak;
makes thin the divide between here and the Other Place.

The witches caw for food.
They love cake; always more cake.

Outside where the air is midnight black,
Big Woman stumbles her way to the well
to draw up the water for mixing.

She has only a sieve to carry, and knows
that the task means her death.

Stretching her two arms down,
her tears fall into the pit.

A voice speaks from the shimmering hole;
"Yellow clay and moss
will bind the sieve like plaster."

So she does.

She delivers the mix to the witches,
who send her outside in the dark,
to stand like a child failing in class.

In the house, crusted with dreams,
the witches collect blood from each sleeping child,
and sweeten the cake with their takings.

● ● ●

Out by the well again,
the voice of the water speaks clear:

"When you come to the north of the house, bellow three times
that the mountain of Fennian women is burning,
and the sky above is on fire."

At the northern end of the house,
she brays hard the message three times.

From the door burst the witches, amok,
in terror, smeared with licks of wool

in the loose, cold air, floating
around them, like soft sparks of light.

They flee.

The voice continues to speak
from the ghost-hole,
the glimmered-pit,
this gaped slit that reaches down,

down past slippery tree roots,
past the crumbling bones of the Celts,
the brassy shingle of dragon scales,

to that smoky conscience
that grinds in the heart of the earth.

"These are old forces
you have allowed into your house.

You must re-enter that place this second;
you need to carry a bold shoulder of power
to block the flank of their magics.

Sprinkle the threshold with water
in which you have washed the feet of your children.
Take crumbs of the cake the horned ones made
with blood from your sleeping family.

Break the cake and drop crumbs in their sleeping mouths,
this will break evil and restore them.

Two final hexes:
Take their cloth and place it half in and half out
of a chest you then bind and lock tight.

Place a great crossbeam across the doors,
that no pagan muscle can shift."

• • •

Time passes.
Just when the Big Woman is moved toward forgetting,
the baleful coven returns.

A batter-thrash on the door: the gurgling shriek,
the twelve crones gathered,
horns glinty and steaming,
crows circling in the iron piss rain,
a chant that bullies its demands.

The foot-water speaks:
"No entry here for you. None.
I am scattered across this threshold.

I hold the power of the loch, the river, the clouds;
the dew in the grass, the weeping of women;
I will block such queer folk as you."

Then the door speaks:
"A beam like iron strides my storied oak.

I am a collision for you wintery spirits.
With my hearth-fire power,
I will outlast you with this simple twig."

The twelve send a thin croon
to the spirit of the blood-bread,
their greatest power in the house.

"Spirit that holds the family blood,
open this door, break beam and water."

"I cannot. My round shape has been quartered,
crumbled, and placed in the mouths of the children.
Your spell-cant is turned widdershins
and your powers are cockless."

The shrieking ensemble
will not leave the scene.
All their strange persuasions, they try.

But this is an island of the strong door,
that carries the truth of a boar's tusks,
a Dingle wave's salty defiance,
and they can do nothing.

Before dawn they slip away.

In the light of morning comes safety.
The Big Woman steps from her house
and twitches her nose in the bruise-fresh air.

There is a dropped mantle left
in the thick ruts of the muddy-hoofed lane;
no witching this time, just haste.

For five hundred years now the mantle has hung
on a rusty nail in the Old Place.

As a reminder of what lingers
in the fields and the lanes,
when the house sleeps,

and rain sleets the glass.

THE OWL-COURT OF IFOR HAEL

Welsh, by Evan Evans, 1731–1788

This eerie ruin among the alders,
this ghostly hump of bramble and thorn,

was once the court of Ifor Hael.

Boys don't make
their stick-dens here.

The thrush and badger
are discreet visitors

in a low-lying fog,
or at dawn's yellow glitter.

Where are the poets?
the bard and storied-harp?

or the generous lord,
with a cup of wine at his arm?

For Dafydd,
chief of the skilled singers,

it was a bleak woe
to lay Ifor in the slick clay.

As he lit the red candles,
and the snow wetted his beard,

then Dafydd knew
that the game was up.

This used to be a welcome ground,
a broad thoroughfare of song,

but is now an owl-court
for those lost in the forest.

For all fame's
beating of shields

there are no ramparts here
jutting through this ivy,

just a moon-blue cry
from the thin, black branches.

WHO WILL BUY A POEM?

Irish, by Mahon O'Heffernan, early seventeenth century

I ask you, who will buy a poem?
Stuffed full of a sage's learning?
Won't anyone take a noble poem
that would make them immortal?

Close-knit as a riddle, true as the law
my poem is,
but I have trudged from cross to cross
of every marketplace in Munster
and it has brought me no profit.

A groat would be a feeble exchange,
but no woman or man has offered me that.
Not Irish or English took notice
of its nimble reasoning.

This is not an art I can profit from,
but it's hard that it should die out.

Yet I am coming to believe
there's more dignity in making combs
to sell at market
than poetry.

The Great Ones—like Corc of Cashel—
they were no hoarders.
They rewarded their poets
with cattle and gold.

It is in vain, this quest I'm on.

I am a trading ship that has lost its freight.

THE HERMIT'S HUT

Irish, author unknown, tenth century

I'm well hidden,
no one but God knows my hut;
enclosed by ash, hazel and heathery mounds.

Lintel of honeysuckle, doorposts of oak;
and the woods thick with nuts
for the fattening pigs.

My small hut on a path
smoothed by my own feet
is crowned by the song
of the blackbird in the gable.

It's just a wee hut,
but it owns the whole forest;
will you go with me to see it?

From such a place
you can see red Roighne, noble Mucraimhe,
and majestic Maenmhagh,
and my view of the meadow is a green joy.

Water gushes from spring to my own happy cup,
the stags of Druim Rolach leap over my stream.
Swine and wild goats, and the badger's plump brood.
All nature stays close
to such refreshment.

I make mead from this honey
and the good hazel-bush,
I make beer with scented herbs.

There is no quarrel here, no hour of strife.
Bright song of the swan, be with me always,

and the nimble wren in the hazel bough,
and swarms of bees, and wild geese.
The wind in the pines makes music sweeter
than any harpist.

I know where a patch of strawberries grows.

How could I not think
that God has sent these things to me?

THE END OF THINGS

Irish, author unknown, twelfth century

Bitter death
is clenched between my teeth.

But a greater bitterness will meet
the ones who come next.

There will not be another king
to unfold the swan-feather cloak of justice,

or to scatter sun-blond loaves
amongst the starving.

There will be no lean bishop
to praise the altar,

no landsman to steward
the herds of milk-fat cattle.

Those strong elders
who held Christ's words like flame

cupped in their strong hands

were resolute, and clear,
not fat with beer and venison.

Learned men, in service to
the King of the Sun,

men who did not place their hands
on handsome boys or fulsome women.

Their nature washed clean
by waterfall and word.

Itchy shirt
Rough cloak
Tough rules.

Such were the nettle-beds they lay in.

Those that are coming
are soured milk.

Swollen with gold, cattle,
plunder and chessboards.

With silk and satin,
they garnish their frames.

When loose with drink,
they reach for the young.

They stagger toward beds
to nest with dark spirits.

These slippery ones
may take the shape of gods.

They may seem immense,
like storms, or mountain eagles.

They may grip our villages
in their ringed fists.

But they will fade

as grass fades in the winter,
they will slip under.

Like the flowers of the field,
like young corn, they will fade.

Their false path
is a serpent's track

and will lead them soon, with their gold cups,
into bitter torments.

Ah yes.
Death is between my teeth.

PRAISE TO ARTHUR'S HIDDEN MEN

Welsh, author unknown, tenth century

Under snow-bent trees
        and by wintering fire,
                I rise and give praise;

to Morfan, son of Tegid,
        so robust in his ugliness,
                no weapon dared strike him

not even in the battle of Camlan,
        as all thought he was servant to a demon.

A river of hair roamed his face;
        moon-yellow teeth;
                a cornered bull.

He fought at Camlan,
        alongside Sandde Angel-Face,
so handsome a man
        no spear came his way
                as all thought he was servant to an angel.

I send a voice in this ice-dark:

to Henwas the Winged, son of Erim,

Henbeddestr son of Erim,

Scilti the Lightfooted, son of Erim.

All three were wind and blur,
        never taking a track when they
                could gallop over a crest of trees,
leap the gray mountain,
        skim the green stream.

Their whole lives,
        not one rush was bent under their foot.

My heart flushes too
      with the name of Teithi the Old,
           son of Gwynham,

whose coast-bold castle
        was shouldered into sand
            by the teeth of the sea.

Who came to Arthur,
        was gathered in, welcomed to table,

but whose arm was swift to anger
      a man not fit for peace and rest,

and for that reason
     grew sick with a gloom,
         that took him down.

Ah, and Drem, son of Dremidydd,
        the Big Seer,

his roaming vision loped from Celli Wig in Cornwall,
    to the black north of Penn Blathaon
                in Scotland.

He could spy one green bud
        under the hoarfrost
           a hundred miles away.

He was firm with usefulness.

Osla of the Big Knife,
        the one who placed his vast sheathed blade
          across any river that blocked Arthur's path.

A sterling bridge
        for the army of the three kingdoms of Britain.

I raise language to
     Gilla Stag-Leg
          that one who leapt
three hundred acres in
         one swift bound.

Lord, I remember
     The vast-bellied Erwm and Hir Atrwm,

and how we would have to raid
        three hundred townships just to feed them.

They would feast steady till noon,
        and blaze up again at dusk,
           shaking their goblets.

When they staggered to bed, they yanked off the heads
     of any wandering vermin,
          as if no chop had ever glazed their lips.

They took the fat, they took the lean,
they took the hot, they took the cold,
they took the sour, they took the sweet,
they took the fresh, they took the salted.

If I quiet now, I think I can hear them chomping still.

Sol, Gwaddn Osol, and Gwaddn of the Bonfire,
       that riotous bunch,
           I raise the glass and remember—

Gwallgoig too.
     Many a village is sleep-sore from his revels.

Sugn, son of Sugnedudd,
       so plagued by heartburn
              that he would suck up the ocean

with three hundred proud ships afloat,
         and gulp it down,
             till there was nothing but a dry stand.

Beloved Cachamwri,
       Arthur's own servant,

with his terrible iron flail,
       who could take a barn,
          robust with thirty ploughs,

and grind the crossbeams and the posts
       and the rafters
         to nothing but oat-size crumbs on the floor,

no friend of farmers.

Gwefl, son of Gwastad,
       our true Grief Man;

When in his blue dream,
       he would let his bottom lip fall to his belly,

and the top he would fit over his head
            as a cap.

A sorrowed mouth, big enough for the world's tears.

Uchdryd of the Cross-Beard,
       who would wrap his bristly red beard
         clear over the fifty rafters of Arthur's Hall,

insulation for a sheep-white winter.

Clust, son of Clustfeinad:
                even when we buried him,
                                seven leagues under dark soil,

he could hear an ant wander
        fifty miles away, leaving its lair.

Ah, Medr son of Medredydd,
                Gwiawan Cat's Eye,
                        Cynyr of the Beautiful Beard—

do you think we have forgotten you?

Listen across the Crow River at my speech.

Medr, who could shoot a wren
                right through its two legs.

Gwiawan, who could cut the lid
        from the eye of a gnat without hurting it.

Cynyr, of whom it is rumored
                great Cai is his son.

And what of Cai?
                Cai of the strange gifting.

Nine nights and nine days he could lie
                under the breathless waters,

                        a moon-track on the sea bed.

Nine nights and nine days he could live
                without sleep.

No doctor could cure a sword-cut
                delivered by Cai.

He was a man of high skill,
        as tall as the wood's highest tree when he chose.

When caught by storm,
        such was his body's heat
            that a whole circle around him would remain dry.

When frozen in the iron-numb
            gullies of Snowdon,
                    we would gather close
                round Cai to dry our kindling.

Great ones, are you safely gathered in?

Let wild fawn
        always be at your bow.
Let your white-bronze rings and broaches
        glow by the yellow candle.
Let the women
        with the dark river hair
                be your companions.

And I,
        with my few wintered logs,

alone and old,
        on the snowy hill

with nothing left
        but my praise.

AFTERWORD:
SOME NOTES ON CONTEXT AND PROCESS

1. The Bards

The Irish bards, it seems, had schools in which young men, if they had an inclination, could study to become poets. These bardic training schools instructed the students in poetic technique, in the strengthening of memory and in the cultivation of imagination. The training included annual examinations. Assigned a theme and a complex set of prosodic requirements, the young men would retire to special huts or cells, rooms entirely lacking in windows, lamps or distraction. There, in the pitch-black, they would lie on their plain wooden beds, and slowly compose their poem, a text written and revised entirely in memory. The last account of such a school can be found in the *Memoirs of the Marquis of Clanricarde*, written in 1641–1643:

> The students, having been given over Night, they work'd it apart each
> by himself upon his own Bed, the whole next Day in the Dark, till at
> a certain Hour in the Night, Lights being brought in, they committed
> it to writing.

For a full night and a day, the poet would lie in that dark, thinking, muttering to himself, composing, revising, and repeating. On the second night, when the poem was due to be delivered in its entirety, an assistant would enter the room with a lamp; only then would the poem be committed to ink and paper. The students were then escorted to a common hall to recite their poem to the master-laureate. The process might take days; hardship was part of the making. According to other accounts of Gaelic composition in the Middle Ages, bards would lie on the ground, with a heavy stone on their bellies for help with their concentration.

The last of these bardic schools probably disappeared in the seventeenth century, when most of the scant remaining Gaelic aristocracy were displaced by English rule. The professional caste of poets, along with the aristocratic system of patronage that sustained them, gradually degraded and disintegrated, along with the culture and language it belonged to. From that time on, poems and stories would for the most part be composed and recorded in written language.

2. An Improbable Endurance

Celtic literature has been subject to so many such interruptions, transformations, and assaults over its history, it is a wonder that any of it remains. As an initially entirely oral literature—therefore alive only in the memory of particular individuals—it was especially fragile and vulnerable to being lost. "I doubt," says the writer and scholar Frank O'Connor, "if ten or even five percent of the literature has come down to us in anything like its original form." In the constant instabilities of the Middle Ages—invasions, migrations, ideological displacements, and linguistic changes—most poems and stories vanished forever; others were only raggedly preserved; many others have been transcribed and changed in the process, then transcribed and changed again. Truthfully, *Cinderbiter: Celtic Poems* represents one more iteration in that history of preservation, resurrection, and revivification, one Martin Shaw and I hope will extend the lifespan of this vital literature.

3. Five Years Ago

Five years ago, when the British storyteller and mythologist Martin Shaw sent me his version of the old Celtic tale "Cinderbiter," it set me on my heels. I was amazed by the surging, robust language and virility of the language-palate at work, the life pulsing through its old archaic skin. Rilke says that summer days are like wine still plunged deep in the grape, and Shaw's version of "Cinderbiter" seemed similarly plunged deep in the romance of language and legend, something very different from the American tradition I belong to. In the best way, it seemed like a story channeled through rapture. Shaw's version opens with this compressed, dizzying lyric sentence of landscape:

> The gray churn, the salted bruise, the green bridle;
> the seal-proud comb around Scotland's skulled coasts.

That sumptuous evocation is cannily followed by a single, plainspoken sentence, which sets down its feet to initiate the linear, more grounded narrative:

> Near it there is a farm.

"Cinderbiter" is an old tale, a tale of a hero-boy who rises from humble anonymity to slay a monster, rescue a kingdom, and marry the king's daughter. But Shaw's telling moves back and forth between narrative and poetry, contains strange digressions, and is furnished with archaic flourishes of language that mark its quilted folkloric origins. Reading it, recognizing its original strangeness, I immediately wondered that this story might be even better delivered with the help of certain free-verse poetic techniques: the imposition of line-breaks, stanzas, and pacing to slow down and dramatize the material. In one of our conversations I suggested that, if he was interested, I could show him what I meant.

Thus our correspondence began, a back and forth across the ocean in more ways than one.

4 . The Celtic Character

There are two broad genres of work included in this collection: the big, shaggy stories like "Cinderbiter," which descend from the Welsh and Irish oral narrative traditions, and the short, intensely personal lyric poems voiced by individual speakers. These latter, more compact lyric forms are different in shape and temper from the stories, but both are drawn from the storehouse of the Celtic medieval literary mind. That is to say, they are image-strong, and possess a robustness that can be attributed to their origins in a literature that had not yet become literary—not yet in touch with the intimidating presence of the classical tradition imported by the Roman conquest of the British Isles, or even the idea of fixed authorial texts. This medieval Celtic work possessed what O'Connor describes as "the confidence of a young literature," bold in the process of inventing itself out of an unprecedented milieu. Medieval Celtic poetry, in addition, is saturated with the rare energy of an era when humankind was still intimately connected to nature itself, and to an ongoing faith in the reality of the supernatural.

5. Some History

Merely to itemize the succession of disruptions that transformed these cultures might give the modern reader some idea of the scale and confusion of displacements that were the environment of Celtic literature.

In the third century, the Roman Empire invaded and entered Britannia. Consequently, in the fourth and fifth centuries, the old Celtic cultures of Ireland, Scotland, and Wales were pressured from the south and east by the recently Romanized Britannic cultures of what we now know as Great Britain. These invaders brought with them the Hellenic culture of

Southern Europe that we call Classical. At the same time, if at a different speed, the conquerors brought with them Christianity in the form of the Roman Catholic Church, which infiltrated the Celtic world of Ireland and Wales more effectively than the Roman militias. Along with religion, that infiltration brought another, perhaps even more profound transformative agent—literacy and written literature.

In the fifth century the collapse of the Empire caused the Romans to withdraw, but they left behind their gift of written literature, a storehouse of knowledge fixed in print on pages, an immensely expanded worldview, the foundations of rational humanism, and a hierarchical conception of civilization. Against these powerful homogenizing agencies of civilization, the peripheral Celtic cultures survived and resisted, even while being influenced.

In the ninth century, however, the Celtic territories were regularly raided from the north by the Danish warriors we know as Vikings. Once again, the Celtic world was destabilized, abraded and changed. From the Danes, however, on a literary level, came the literary infusion of the Sagas and Eddas, the warrior-culture celebrated in tales of Beowulf and Cuchulain.

The Norman Conquest in the eleventh century brought the influence and forms of French and Continental culture into Britain, gradually developing into the colonization of the Celtic world by the English feudal system. These incursions would eventually mean the deterioration of the Celtic poet system and of the Celtic languages themselves.

6. The One Fact to Understand

If there is a single fact for the modern reader to understand about this rich body of literature, it is the double consciousness embodied in most of these poems and stories. That layered heterogeneity is a consequence of the many crosshatched legacies described above: warrior songs, prayers of Christian asceticism, ecstatic poems of pagan pantheism, and monologues of solitary wanderers. Within these pieces, such seemingly contradictory impulses display no awareness of internal conflict. The old gods and new gods coexist, to which can be added the Latin of Christianity and the organized governance that made the Roman Empire the supreme civilization that it was.

A parallel complexity is to be found in the verbal sensibility, the various linguistic character of many of the lyric poems: a love of linguistic alliterative glamor and elegance. Some of them are laden with the sonic beauty and muscular embellishments of oral Celtic instincts; some are stripped down to the plainsong of prayer.

The poem "The Mansion of the Woods" in this collection offers one example of the paradoxical coexistence of Christian reverence alongside an older, rapturous pantheism. Though written near the end of the medieval period, by a devout Welsh priest named Edmund Price, the poem is un-self-consciously full of nature worship. The poem is a love song to the birds, "the glad fellows of the branch," the

Nightingale of the lovers;
blackbird loose with zeal;
woodlark adrift with wanton speech;
linnet preaching from the brake.

Here, nature itself holds the status of the divine. The sensuous, self-pleasuring language of the poem embodies an almost erotic intimacy with nature that we can sense and envy.

As previously suggested, the unconflicted coexistence of two systems in much Celtic poetry is usually attributed to historical circumstances: the overlapping layers of indigenous and invasive cultures and languages. When the Roman Empire withdrew its perimeter from Britannia, it left Irish monasteries and believers on their own for centuries. Much like a species of animal in geographic isolation, Irish Christianity developed its own peculiarities, including a sensibility of great asceticism and devoutness. Yet that strict devotion did not exclude the indigenous radiant Celtic imagination. Many of these poems bear the mark of such mixed bilateral allegiances.

As Price says, "In this glade, all is drawn up together, / intermingled, commingling." Such intermingled allegiances make it possible for the poet to praise alternately the Roman female deity Venus and "the strange bounty" of "the Father" within the space of a few lines:

No trouble is here, no sickness;
Venus owns this Bright Mansion.

Drag to this place
all crippled in spirit
both young and old.

What strange bounty the Father sings!
His tone strong-backed with wheat,
and glimmered with barley
on the horn-clear hills.

The tone is a mixture of the religious, the erotic, and the ecstatic. The poem itself sails along with un-self-conscious freshness.

7. The Stories

Another legacy of the complex, split identity of these works can be seen in the long stories gathered here: "Bard-Come-a-Fire," "Fionn's Migrations," "Blodeuedd of the Owl-Face." These stories are rife with the richness of folklore, the tradition of hero-narratives, the fantastic litigations of mortals with supernatural forces, the warrior ethics of tribal and Viking cultures, and Christianity as well.

Each story itself is a "hero's journey" of self-development, but the supernatural plays a primary, often fantastical role closer to the genres of folktale and legend than gospel. The schooling of the hero that often takes place is the tutorial of learning cooperation with the invisible powers of the underworld, magicians and entities far different from any Christian hierarchy. In these tales, it is the courage and development of the warrior hero that preoccupies the poem, rather than the cultivation of virtue and duty to God. Accordingly, these poems resolve in ways that resemble the plot of Viking sagas, with the ascension of a hero to kingship and fame, not to sainthood.

8. "Bard-Come-a-Fire"

No story collected here is more unclassifiable and fantastic than the story-poem titled "Bard-Come-a-Fire," which embodies many of the hybrid complexities of this literature. The materials of this version are drawn from Geoffrey of Monmouth's *Vita Merlini*, transcribed in Latin in the twelfth century from ancient Welsh sources. "Bard-Come-a-Fire" features the figure that has come down to us as Merlin the magician. But here, the figure of Merlin is an inscrutable and protean cipher-figure, more shaman than guardian.

Merlin is designated a "bard" in the story's title, but in fact he embodies the whole spectrum of poetic duties and gifts. Initially we are told that he is a tutor for the children of nobility; subsequently he is a player in the exercise of martial might; capable of powerful curses in battle. In still another dimension, this Merlin-figure occupies a pagan druidic position; he stands in the liminal area between nature and humanity, between humanity and the cosmos, and mediates between them. We are told that he communicates with creatures, plants, and weather. In the second half of this wild story, Merlin suffers a psychological breakdown, flees the violence of humanity—and disappears into the woods, where, for years, his identity is given over to the wild—the animals and the natural vegetative deities.

By the conclusion of "Bard-Come-a-Fire" the Merlin figure is ultimately aloof from and skeptical of the concerns of human civilization. His mysterious figure is, in fact, an antithesis to the Christian culture which places humankind at its center. To read such a story is disorienting even today, with its chaotic narrative permutations. We may seek for conventional elements of psychology or moral theme, but such meridians do not exactly fit when encountering such ungoverned old imagination. The Arthur stories we are familiar with are clothed in Christian ethos, but here Merlin is a figure from outside, who traffics with pagan realities on behalf of his culture—finally as ungovernable as the old gods.

9. The Lyric Poems

If the stories like "Bard-Come-a-Fire" and "Blodeuedd of the Owl-Face" are sprawling supernatural narratives quilted together from many tellings, the lyric poems in this collection are more inward-looking and personal, more intimate in tone, and also more depressed and sorrowful. In contrast to the burly, supernaturally sparked tales, these lyric dramatic monologues speak from the ground of personal experience, the individual struggling and enduring in time.

Often set against a backdrop of a withering culture, poems like "The Ruins of Timoleague Abbey" and "Hut Talk" describe monasteries abandoned in ruins, both monks and patronage disappeared. Their speakers are hermits or wanderers who nostalgically view the remains of a once-flourishing religious culture. In part, these broken landscapes of ruined monastic edifices are simply historical representations. The Viking and Norman invasions of the ninth to eleventh centuries dismantled the economic infrastructure of the Roman church that supported such monasteries.

Yet O'Connor says that this "backwards look" is also a characteristic part of the Celtic temperament. In any case, these lyric poems of heartbreak and wandering found in poems like "Deirdre Remembers a Scottish Glen" personalize dimensions of the historical literature. They make more intimate while also widening the lens we peer through.

Here too we frequently find a double consciousness: freed from the designs of human intention, the landscapes that remain are a kind of overgrown Eden, a green, animate creation that manifests no separateness from the human spectator. The monologue "The Wild Man and the Monastery," perhaps spoken by a former novitiate, itemizes the contrast between the spiritual willfulness of sanctioned religion and the old communion with nature itself:

> There was an age,
> an age
> when sweeter for me
> than the hum of monks
>
> was the coo-call
> of the ringdove
> flitting above
> the gray pool.
>
> An age when sweeter
> than the tinkling call to prayer
> was the blackbirds' warble
>
> in the dusty gable
> and the stag's dark belling
> in the storm.

Though the wild man's poem is cast in a nostalgic-sounding past tense, what the poem makes clear is that the speaker's pagan allegiances are hardly extinguished. The poet's images have the distinctive vividness, passion and intimacy characteristic of the Celtic. As the wild man's poem concludes:

> These fattened monks
> are swift to ale,
> but I like better

ice-water cupped
from the
green spring.

10. Who Were These Poets? The Social Background

This essay began by describing the grueling regimen of the bardic schools, and some brief discussion is required to sketch out more of the circumstances of the old poets. Who were these poets who composed and or transmitted these poems and stories? They themselves had an array of caste identities, social functions, and means of livelihood. Some were professional poets retained by patrons, who primarily served a tribal lord or court.

Such a poet or bard may have resided in the court of a fifth century Welsh nobleman, earning his retainer as a poetic keeper of the family genealogy and as a sort of public relations agent in charge of recording and embellishing his patron's illustrious deeds. A few poems in this collection, like "Who Will Buy a Poem?" and "Lament of the Four MacDonalds," make reference to the patron system, as well as lamenting the decline of the families that they served.

These professional poets were well rewarded for their services; in exchange for a poem of praise for his patron, the poet might be given twenty or thirty cattle or even a farm. These bards, or *fili*, had a high place in society, one roughly parallel to the class of pagan druids which preceded Christianity, or following the Christianization of Britannia, a status equivalent to that of an esteemed priest. The bard's duties were secular, sacred, and martial; to a lord or chieftain, a poet was an essential ally to the achievement and maintenance of fame and repute. In addition, poets were thought, through their powers of satire, capable of bringing death and dishonor to an enemy or a stingy patron. The bard himself had a kind of entourage, consisting of a harpist and a reciter of the poem; these retainers themselves were profitably rewarded for their role in the performance and perpetuation of poems. From the distance of our modern perspective, it is a little difficult to credit the power accorded to the medieval spoken and written word.

Another class of bard was the traveling, more populist hearth poet, who would have wandered the countryside from village and town, reciting his tales for country folk. Such stories had no fixed authorship; they were retained in memory and through retelling upon retelling. Stories like "Cinderbiter" belonged to the culture, and to folklore, and to the society of oral singers, who embellished, subtracted, and added to the base templates of the tales, transmuting them in the telling. In this collection, those stories, though apparently fixed in print on a page, are simply finding one more iteration in their fluid history. The big, hurly-burly stories like "Cinderbiter" or "The Horned Women" probably belonged to this tradition of traveling communal storytellers, the hearth poets, who transported and recited these tales.

11. The Oral Context for This Work

For modern readers, of course, the story of oral literature is conventionally set against the backdrop of written literature. But that metaphor itself is misleading. Our modern literary imagination has been schooled by the assumption of fixed and definitive texts, texts "committed" to paper, with the names of authors and publishers embossed upon their title pages. In that archived value system, written texts are recognized as the absolute foundation of a given culture.

In fact, however, we should think of written literature as positioned against the deep and fluid background of oral traditions and the background of archetype itself. Imagine a verbal universe that existed entirely in its passage between mouth and ears, never separate from the gestural language of a living speaker and the changing pitch and pace of a human voice; a knitted, knitting thing that was, nonetheless, as important and substantial as human imagination itself. It may seem "exotic" from our perspective, but these oral recitations and performances also had, from their beginning, intensely pragmatic civic functions: to publicly formalize the legal contracts that governed citizens and social structures, to secure medical knowledge in the collective memory, and to reiterate community histories.

Such cultures were critically sustained and nourished—as is our own, of course—by their own speech, by the verbal imagination of their stories and poems—their entertainments. The heroic legends and origin myths, the tales of the supernatural, of geography and genealogy, bound communities into their identities in ways that made survival possible. The social performance, repetition, and reception of poems and stories in a preliterate culture were crucially culture-making.

12. Translation

Translation is a controversial enterprise, and in our historically, politically self-conscious era, more so now than ever. The perennial question is: "Is this a betrayal of the original culture?" That question seems formulated more aggressively today as: "Is this an insensitive form of literary colonialism?" But such questions, though useful, halt us more than guide us. The wise scholar Burton Raffel, in his introduction to his own translations from Old English, describes both pragmatical and spiritual aspects of the enterprise:

> It can almost never be successful as a task. . . . The translator's only hope is to re-create something roughly equivalent in the new language, something that is itself good poetry and that at the same time carries a reasonable measure of the force and flavor of the original. In this sense a re-creation can only be a creation. And a creation cannot be simply willed; it must be felt. . . . As a kind of first principle, there plainly must be something in the tone . . . something not only translatable but also already actively present in the general spirit of contemporaneous verse in the translator's own language. . . .
>
> But its only justification is itself, not the original from which it derives. . . . A poem in its own right which can convey at least a part of the savour, the foreign and different savour as well as the similar and known savour, a poem meaningful in its own language and at the same time suggestive of the accents and the culture of another.

Inevitably, the transformation of the originals has been substantial in our work. It could not be otherwise. Celtic lyric poetry was subject to rigorous rules of compression, alliterative prosody, and order that are untransferable to English. In any case, we have worked from translations, or—as in the case of "Cinderbiter"—from stories whose history is one of largely oral transmission, the story altered in each iteration. Original cultures, and the contexts and conditions under which those cultures thrived, are gone. Any possible iteration is a transformation.

As O'Connor says, "though scholars are voracious always for an ur, original text . . . from which everything descends . . . there was never such a thing as an original in our sense of the word. . . . Irish men of letters in the early Middle Ages had no conception of authorship or of a text as a thing in itself, and felt perfectly free to add, subtract, and rewrite." Part of their radiance, says O'Connor, is that they were never beaten into shape by any dominating literary intelligence who could impose his versions on his successors: "though they are literature, they retain the wavering, uncertain quality of folklore with its innumerable forgotten authors."

As mentioned earlier, the lyric poems in this collection are drawn from the invaluable 1951 translations done by the scholar Kenneth Hurlstone Jackson in the anthology *A Celtic Miscellany*. In his preface, Jackson emphasizes that his goals were meticulous fidelity to the originals and unembellished preservation. One can only be grateful for the faithfulness of Jackson's translations. Nonetheless, some freshness of the poems seems often to be lost, or muted, by his obligation to exactitude and thoroughness. Additionally, the renditions seemed, in their lengthiness, unsuited for a contemporary audience. Exhaustively rendered into prose paragraphs, Jackson's versions can be at times redundant and lyrically shapeless.

Our recast versions reflect a desire to accent some of the luscious resonance of the imagery and speech, while abbreviating and shaping the lyrics. These new versions of the poems have been additionally embellished, lineated, amplified, and changed for dramatic shape and lyric balance.

A good example of the shaping process we have engaged in might be found in the lyric Welsh poem by Dafydd ap Gwilym, "The Girls of Llanbadorn." From the 1300s, the poem is a monologue spoken by a young man—his irreverent, self-consciously roguish complaint about his bad romantic luck. First, consider a portion of Jackson's carefully prosed version of the poem in *A Celtic Miscellany*:

I am twisted with passion—plague on all the girls of the parish! since I suffered from trysts which went amiss, and could never win a single one of them, neither gentle hopeful maid, nor little lass, nor hag, nor wife. What fright is this, what mischief, what failure, that they'll have none of me? What harm could it be for a fine-browed maiden to meet me in the thick dark wood? It would be no shame to her to see me in my leafy lair. There has never been a time when I did not fall in love with one or two in a single day; there was never a spell so persistent as this, not even on those as passionate as Garwy. Yet for all that I was no nearer to winning one of them, than if she were my enemy.

The leaner, shaped version of the poem we have produced in *Cinderbiter* organizes and paces this narrative monologue into a dramatic sequence of declarative statements. Clearly, it is a substantial alteration of the original text; but the compression and selection strengthen the images, and in this case, we think, also renders the young man's voice as something edgier and more psychologically complex than Jackson's version:

Since I was young I have been mad for girls.
One dozen times a day I fall in love.

No Sunday has passed but that I am in the pews at Mass,
in my feathered hat,

my eyes turned keen across the congregation.
But in this parish a curse from God has ruined me.

Neither gentle lass, nor lonely wife, nor cankered hag
will sport with me.

Among themselves, the women say, "View his face;
he has the look of one who knows sin well."

There never was a spell so persistent as this.

My neck has grown cricked from looking left and right,
and still no mate.

I am no more close to winning one of them
than if I was their enemy.

And I must give up these fantasies
and become a hermit, or even worse, a saint.

Not surprisingly, increased economy makes for greater vividness and elicits, or sharpens, a medley of tones in the speaker's voice: not just frustration, but self-caricature, plaintive longing and anxiety. Translation here is not simply an act of fidelity, but a keen retuning of the poem to a contemporary psychological representation. When one considers the long passage, and many veils through which the poem has travelled from Welsh of the fourteenth century to English of the twenty-first century, the clarity and freshness of the poem, its lack of strangeness, seems a miracle of transportation.

Other models for such adaptations abound, from Seamus Heaney's *Beowulf* to Christopher Logue's seizure and amplification of select moments in the text of *The Iliad* in his book *War Music*. Mary Jo Bang translated Dante's *Inferno* into a kind of punk slang. Ours is an era of sometimes reckless literary transmogrifying. If at times the results are hybrid and strange, the best efforts have made poetry that preserves the elegance, antiquity, and force of the original and at the same time contemporizes it.

This form of reconstitution may be imperfect—to some, perhaps, even heretical—and yet it is not disrespectful. We see our versions as a rehydration, a form of yearning, a recognition of value, and a reaching back into the dark to pull up something culture has lost, for restoration. However flawed our efforts, we feel that the wild, distinctive spirit of the poems and stories has been preserved and extended, that it is genuinely alive. In making this collection, we are turning these Celtic poems loose one more time, to roam, we hope, far into the future.

Tony Hoagland
Santa Fe, New Mexico
2018

MARTIN SHAW is a mythologist, storyteller, author, and director of the Westcountry School of Myth in the United Kingdom. He is the author of *A Branch from the Lightning Tree: Ecstatic Myth and the Grace of Wildness*, *Snowy Tower: Parzival and the Wet Black Branch of Language*, *Scatterlings: Getting Claimed in the Age of Amnesia*, *The Night Wages*, *Wolf Milk: Chthonic Memory in the Deep Wild*, and *Elk Bone Is a Bright Owl*, and cotranslator of *Courting the Dawn: Poems of Lorca* with Stephan Harding. Shaw is also the author of "Myth in Real Time: An Essay and Conversation with Ai Weiwei," featured in Ai Weiwei's *Life Cycle*. He regularly teaches at Stanford University and otherwise lives in Devon in the southwest of Britain.

TONY HOAGLAND (1953–2018) was the author of eight books of poetry, including *Priest Turned Therapist Treats Fear of God*; *What Narcissism Means to Me*, a finalist for the National Book Critics Circle Award; and *Donkey Gospel*, winner of the James Laughlin Award of the Academy of American Poets. He was also the author of four works of criticism, including *Twenty Poems That Could Save America and Other Essays* and *The Art of Voice: Poetic Principles and Practice* (with Kay Cosgrove). Hoagland received the Jackson Poetry Prize from Poets & Writers, the Mark Twain Award from the Poetry Foundation, and the O. B. Hardison Jr. Poetry Prize from the Folger Shakespeare Library. He taught for many years at the University of Houston.

The text of *Cinderbiter* is set in Baskerville URW.
Book design by Rachel Holscher.
Composition by Bookmobile Design and Digital Publisher
Services, Minneapolis, Minnesota.
Manufactured by Bookmobile on acid-free, 100 percent
postconsumer wastepaper.